EISENHOWER

MILITARY PROFILES

SERIES EDITOR
Dennis E. Showalter, Ph.D.
Colorado College

*Instructive summaries for general and expert
readers alike, volumes in the Military Profiles
series are essential treatments of significant and
popular military figures drawn from world history,
ancient times through the present.*

EISENHOWER

Soldier-Statesman
of the American Century

Douglas Kinnard

Brassey's, Inc.
Washington, D.C.

Library of Congress Cataloging-in-Publication Data
Kinnard, Douglas.
Eisenhower : soldier-statesman of the American century /
Douglas Kinnard — 1st ed.
p. cm. — (Military profiles)
Includes bibliographical references and index.
ISBN 1-57488-399-2 (alk. paper)
1. Eisenhower, Dwight D. (Dwight David), 1890–1969.
2. Eisenhower, Dwight D. (Dwight David), 1890–1969 —
Career in the military. 3. Eisenhower, Dwight D. (Dwight
David), 1890–1969 — Military leadership. 4. Presidents —
United States — Biography. 5. Generals — United States —
Biography. 6. United States. Army — Biography.
I. Title. II. Series.
E836 .K555 2002
973.921'092 — dc21   202008030

Printed in the United States of America on acid-free paper that meets the American National Standards Institute z39-48 Standard.

Brassey's, Inc.
22841 Quicksilver Drive
Dulles, Virginia 20166

FIRST EDITION

10 9 8 7 6 5 4 3 2 1

To Wade
après cinquante ans

Contents

Preface

Dwight Eisenhower, the last American president to be born in the nineteenth century, was in the center of major world events for two decades in the middle of the twentieth. As a soldier he commanded the Allied armies that defeated the Axis powers. In the following decade he served two terms as a very popular president.

Long before he became a practicing politician, Ike was a professional soldier. He labored in the peacetime "Brown Shoe Army"—the Army in the years between the world wars, where promotion was a rare event. He served directly under Gen. Douglas MacArthur in Washington and Manila, then came to public attention during the great Louisiana field maneuvers of 1941. So impressed was Army Chief of Staff George Marshall that he later jumped Eisenhower over several hundred shocked senior generals to eventual command of Allied forces in the Mediterranean.

His subsequent selection as Supreme Commander of the Allied invasion of northern Europe—Operation Overlord—projected him onto the world scene. No other American general ever had, or probably ever will have, a position of that magnitude. Eisenhower's superb leadership welded the armies of many Western nations into a single coherent fighting force that, along with Soviet forces, ended the Nazi terror. This historic accomplishment made Eisenhower the symbol of that glorious victory.

Notwithstanding his fame, he was still Ike of the big grin, increasingly beloved by Americans. After the war in Europe he came home to be Army Chief of Staff, usually the capstone of an Army career, but in this case an anticlimax. From Washington he moved to New York as president of Columbia University. Then in 1950 duty called again. In the wake of the Korean War, at first perceived as part of a worldwide Communist offensive, the North Atlantic Treaty Organization (NATO) needed a supreme commander; they turned to Eisenhower, the old wartime hero. When rumors abounded that he would run for president, the denials became fewer until, in 1952, Eisenhower announced his candidacy. He beat Sen. Robert Taft of Ohio for the nomination in July 1952 on the first ballot, and went on to defeat the cerebral Democratic candidate, Gov. Adlai Stevenson of Illinois, in November. Four years later he faced Stevenson again with the same results.

At the end of his eight-year presidency Eisenhower had good reason to feel that the country was better off than it had been when he took the oath of office in 1953. Certainly that was true in terms of Americans' personal income and living standards. He had also improved the general tranquillity of the country by helping to calm the partisan wrangling of the late 1940s and early 1950s. In the field of civil rights his legacy was mixed.

Ike's greatest achievements as president came in the area of foreign policy and related defense matters. He ended the Korean War, avoided a confrontation with China over the offshore islands, and defused the 1956 Suez crisis. In other regions, most notably Cuba and Vietnam, he was not as successful, leaving his less-experienced successor problems that would continue for many years.

The 1950s were a dangerous decade in the Cold War with proliferating weapons increasing the potential for a nuclear exchange with the Soviet Union. Eisenhower handled that challenge superbly, ignoring occasional advice to use nuclear weapons. Despite all his efforts, though, he was unable to achieve any real détente with the USSR.

Dwight Eisenhower was unique among leaders of his time. His face more often expressed his feelings than masked them, though he could muster appropriate reserve when necessary. He could never have emulated Franklin Delano Roosevelt's patrician jocularity or the characteristics of his other contemporaries: the bulldog tenacity of Winston Churchill, the consuming pride of

Douglas MacArthur, the near-arrogance of Charles de Gaulle. One thing Ike's face always showed was genuineness, not the plasticity of a practiced politician. He was truly a man of the people, one of America's most loved twentieth-century men as well as one of the greatest presidents of his century.

So many individuals have provided help and support on my Eisenhower research over the past thirty years that it would be impossible to list all of them here. Working closely with me throughout this project were three persons: Joanne Garland, who after five years of association has become expert at deciphering my frequently illegible handwriting and producing a manuscript; Mary Mitiguy, who has worked with me as editor and adviser for the past twenty-five years; and my wife, Dr. Wade Tyree, who served again as senior editor and critic, and who has also worked with me as a research associate at the Eisenhower Library at Abilene on an earlier Eisenhower book.

Maps

Chronology

1890	Born, Denison, Texas, October 14. Parents: Ida and David Eisenhower.
1891	Family returns to Abilene, Kansas.
1911	Enters West Point.
1915	Graduates from West Point. Commissioned second lieutenant of infantry. Assigned to Fort Sam Houston, Texas.
1916	Marries Mamie Geneva Doud in Denver, July 1.
1918	Commander, Tank Training Center, Camp Colt, Gettysburg, Pennsylvania. In 1918 awarded Distinguished Service Medal.
1922	Becomes executive officer to Gen. Fox Conner, Panama Canal Zone. Second son, John, born August (first son, Icky, born 1917, died 1921).
1926	Graduates first in his class from Command and General Staff School.
1933	Assigned as assistant to Gen. Douglas MacArthur, Chief of Staff, U.S. Army.
1935	Named senior assistant to General MacArthur, military adviser to the Commonwealth of the Philippines.
1940	Joins 15th Infantry Regiment in February as executive officer, later Chief of Staff of Third Division.
1941	Chief of Staff for Ninth Army Corps. Made Chief of Staff for Lt. Gen. Walter Krueger, commander of the Third Army at Fort Sam Houston, Texas. Promoted to brigadier general. Assigned to Washington, D.C., as Assistant Chief of Staff, War Plans Division, under General Marshall.

1942   Promoted to major general. Appointed commander of the European Theater of Operations on June 15. Promoted to lieutenant general in July. Commands Allied invasion of North Africa in November.

1943   Promoted to general. Directs invasion of Sicily in July and August. Launches Italian campaign in September. Appointed supreme commander of Allied Expeditionary Forces in December.

1944   Arrives in London in January to establish Supreme Headquarters. Directs Normandy invasion beginning June 6. Appointed General of the Army in December.

1945   Accepts unconditional surrender of Germany at Reims, France, on May 7. Appears before joint session of Congress on June 18. Becomes commander of U.S. occupation zone of Germany. Returns to Washington, D.C., as Chief of Staff, U.S. Army, November.

1948   Retires as Chief of Staff on May 2. Installed as president of Columbia University on October 12. Publishes *Crusade in Europe*.

1950   Appointed Supreme Commander of North Atlantic Treaty Organization on December 19.

1952   Announces availability as Republican candidate for president in January. Relieved as Supreme Commander in June. Nominated for president by Republicans July 11. Defeats Adlai E. Stevenson November 4.

1953   Inaugurated thirty-fourth president of the United States on January 20.

1956   Announces in February he will run for second term. Wins election on November 6.

1961   Retires to his Gettysburg farm.

1963–65 Publishes memoirs of presidency: *Mandate for Change* and *Waging Peace*.

1969   Dies on March 28 in Walter Reed Army Hospital, Washington, D.C., at age seventy-eight.

EISENHOWER

Chapter 1

Abilene and West Point

"I COME FROM the very heart of America," said Dwight D. Eisenhower on June 12, 1945, as he stood in the medieval splendor of London's Guildhall responding to the Lord Mayor's grant of Freedom of the City. Ike received this ancient honor in gratitude for his service as supreme commander of the Allied forces. Five weeks earlier they had triumphed over the forces of Nazism that for many years had terrorized the European continent and the United Kingdom.

"The very heart of America" was not just rhetoric; Dwight Eisenhower hailed from Abilene, Kansas, twenty miles west of the exact geographic center of the United States. The Eisenhowers, successful Pennsylvania farmers, had arrived in Dickinson County, Kansas, in 1878, drawn to the frontier by railroad publicity and land prices driven downward by an 1870 crash. The family adhered to the teachings of the River Brethren, an offshoot of the German Mennonite sect that began in Zurich in 1528. Their beliefs stressed an agrarian independence from the greater society and an abhorrence of violence and all things military. One family legend, though, held that Eisenhower ancestors (the name meant "iron striker," an evocation of smithery and swordmaking) had ridden horseback as armored warriors in medieval German cohorts.[1]

Always fleeing statist demands and religious persecution, Eisenhowers moved from Bavaria to Switzerland to Holland. Sometime between 1732 and 1741 three Eisenhower brothers arrived in Pennsylvania with a group of River Brethren. With the outbreak of the American Revolution in 1776 the family adopted a more flexible attitude toward their sect's isolation and nonviolence. One forebear, Frederick Eisenhower, distinguished himself as an Indian fighter and later in August 1776 at the Battle of Long Island. Although a staunch pacifist, Ike's grandfather Jacob Eisenhower supported the abolition of slavery; Jacob's brother Samuel rode in the Union Army's Ninth Cavalry.

David, one of Jacob's sons, was fourteen when the family migrated to Kansas. In time he pursued engineering studies at Lane University, a small institution in Lecompton, Kansas. There he met Ida Stover, who had come westward from Virginia's Shenandoah Valley. Married in 1885, they left school and returned to Hope, near Abilene, where Jacob had established a successful farm. David opened a general store underwritten by his father but in a few years came on hard times. Drought and an invasion of grasshoppers beset local farmers, making them unable to pay their bills. David's venture went bankrupt.[2]

At that point he moved Ida and their two sons, Arthur and Edgar, to Dennison, Texas. They settled in a small frame house near the railroad, where David had secured a low-paying job. There a third son, Dwight—known as Ike—was born on October 14, 1890. About that time the River Brethren back in Abilene opened a new creamery and offered David a mechanic's job. Acceptance would mean that the family could return permanently to Kansas. Thus, in the spring of 1891 the Eisenhowers and baby Dwight moved to Abilene, where his three younger brothers were born and the boys grew up.

In that part of Kansas the countryside has not changed much since Ike's boyhood. A driver on Interstate 70 bound west for

Denver or east for St. Louis sees gentle, rolling farmland much as it was a century ago. Before Ike's time Abilene had been a rough cow town, where Texas cowboys brought cattle to the railroads to be shipped east. For a time in 1871 the legendary Wild Bill Hickok had been marshal. During Ike's youth at the turn of the century, though, Abilene, with its population of about four thousand, was a typical small town of rural America. It had no water system until 1902, no paved streets until 1910.

David and Ida brought up Dwight and his brothers in an atmosphere of religion, discipline, and love. The boys had their assigned chores, and woe to the sleepyhead who missed the 5 A.M. starting time. Though poor, the family lived comfortably, raising most of their own food. Besides working at odd jobs, the boys earned money with their vegetable garden. In their hand-me-down clothes they would cart surplus produce to sell in the better-heeled section of town. Adding to the family income still left pocket change for youthful indulgences.

Although instilling obedience and responsibility in her sons, Ida permitted them to fight — as long as they did it outdoors. A quarter-century after Abilene lost its image as a hard-drinking frontier town, Abilene's boys did their best to uphold the fighting tradition. Both "Big Ike" (Edgar) and "Little Ike" (Dwight) grew up as its competent heirs. While keeping up their household duties, Bible study, and school attendance, the Eisenhower boys rounded themselves out at play: Dwight excelled at baseball, football, skating, and — most treasured in the years after high school — poker playing, hunting, and camping.

A popular student, Ike also showed academic strength in mathematics and history. After he and his older brother Edgar graduated together from Abilene High School in 1909, Dwight took a job at the creamery where his father worked. He was helping support Edgar's first-year studies at the University of Michigan; presumably in a following year the tables would be reversed. Ike had in mind Kansas University.

In 1910 an event occurred that would set Dwight on another course. He became a good friend of Swede Hazlett, an Abilene boy studying to retake the Naval Academy's entrance exams that he had failed earlier. Intrigued by the idea of a free education at Annapolis, Ike joined Hazlett in his studies that summer. He applied to Kansas Sen. Joseph L. Bristow, who authorized him to take the competitive exam for the Naval Academy. And, oh yes, the senator also had a vacancy for a place called West Point. After several weeks of cramming, Ike was off to Topeka to take the exam. Ending up second out of eight candidates for the two academies, he received an appointment, not to the Naval Academy but—to his initial disappointment—to West Point.

Dwight Eisenhower now began his first great adventure away from Abilene. On June 14, 1911, he arrived at the tiny West Point railroad station, one of 265 new cadets or, as they were called, plebes. Standing on the plain with the others that afternoon, he held up his right hand to take the oath of allegiance: "I do solemnly swear that I will support the Constitution of the United States. . . ." As he later wrote:

> A feeling came over me that the expression "the United States of America" would now and henceforth mean something different than it ever had before. From here on it would be the nation I would be serving, not myself. [3]

The first weeks, spent in "Beast Barracks," were a period of intense indoctrination designed to fit newcomers into the monastic mold of the academy. The air resounded with cries of "Shoulders back!" "Suck up that gut!" "Chin in, Mr. Dumbjohn!" Each cadet may have been the best athlete, scholar, or all-around boy in his part of the world, but here he was simply a West Point plebe, a member of the Army on the bottom rung. Some cadets could take it; some could not. Ike, although far from being a model cadet, took it in stride. The two years working in Abilene between high school and the Point had made him much more mature and resilient than most of his classmates in enduring the plebe system.

Resilience and maturity aside, Dwight Eisenhower was far from a paradigm in dress gray; he remained a prankster imbued with a Kansan frontier spirit. Once, he and another plebe named

Atkins were commanded to appear at a cadet corporal's room in full-dress uniform. The two plebes complied, wearing only the cutaway tailcoats. The resultant furor moved the two from jokers into victims, but afterward the episode was legendary among their plebe classmates.

When he became an upperclassman himself, hazing had little appeal for Eisenhower. His memoirs tell of an incident in which a plebe bumped into him and fell to the ground. Reacting, Ike told the plebe sarcastically, "You look like a barber." The plebe arose and said softly, "I was a barber, sir." Eisenhower returned to his room embarrassed. Relating the incident to his roommate, he added, "I just did something unforgivable. I made a man ashamed of the work he did." Then he added in the memoir, "Never again did I correct a plebe harshly."[4]

West Point was an engineering school, its curriculum largely technical. Cadet Eisenhower was strong in English but in the technical subjects was content to remain in the middle of the class standings. As he said later, "I was a lazy student." But when he had to be, he was a keen one, as when called upon one day to explain the solution to a problem in integral calculus. Not having memorized the solution, as he was supposed to, he developed his own. Since it was not the approved approach, the instructor demurred, even though Ike had provided a much simpler solution. Fortunately, an associate professor was visiting the class as Ike was explaining his approach. Finding this solution more logical than the approved one, he declared, "We will incorporate it from now on."[5]

In matters of discipline Ike was, in his own words, "far from a good cadet." His infractions were minor, such as smoking in his room or being late in submitting a report, but one caused his reduction from sergeant to private (later he was again a sergeant carrying the colors at parade). That one probably epitomizes the free spirit of the cadet from Abilene: "violation of orders with reference to dancing, having previously been admonished for same." He had substituted a lively turkey trot for the more "respectable" dancing expected of cadets. In discipline Ike ended up number 125 out of the 164 members of his class who graduated. Some biographers attribute his West Point transgressions to his later creativity and success as a commander: the wilder the colt, the faster the thoroughbred, perhaps.

What really motivated Ike was athletics, particularly football, and in the fall of 1912 he made the varsity squad. After the Rutgers game the *New York Times* described him as "one of the most promising backs in Eastern football." The glory was short lived, though. While playing against the Carlisle Indians led by the legendary Jim Thorpe, Ike injured his knee, then against Tufts the following week the injured knee broke. The next week riding drill left the knee a swollen mess and with it the end of Dwight's football career. He contented himself thereafter as a coach for the plebe football team and as a cheerleader, but continued to dine with his former teammates at the training table.

The picture of Ike at West Point lives not only in the official record of Cadet Dwight Eisenhower but also in the memory of those who knew him well in those days. Immensely popular — he liked people and they liked him — he was also able to stimulate cooperation among others, a quality of great importance later on, not just for him but for the nation.[6]

June 12, 1915, was a beautiful day in the Hudson Valley. The 164 cadets of the West Point graduating class, ready to leave those insular halls, sat listening to the speaker, Secretary of War Lindley Garrison, do his duty. It was less beautiful in other places that were, or soon would be, in the news. In Ypres, Gallipoli, and Loos a generation of young men were being slaughtered. In the White House sat Thomas Woodrow Wilson, who was to campaign later that he "kept us out of war." Perhaps more prophetic than the President's boast were the words of Secretary Garrison in telling the graduates: "Be ready to sacrifice all for your country." Soon he presented diplomas to each of the graduates as names were read off. These names included Omar Nelson Bradley, Dwight David Eisenhower, and James Alward Van Fleet. No one could guess then, but one day fifty-nine of them would be generals, and the class of 1915 would become the most famous one in West Point's history: "the class the stars fell on."

Chapter 2

Brown Shoe Army

B<small>Y THE FALL</small> of 1915 the war in Europe that was supposed to have ended in a few months was hopelessly dead-locked, and the butcher's bill was already in the millions. One flank of the Western Front rested on Switzerland, the other on the Flanders seacoast. Neither side was going to outflank the other, and any attempts to break the stalemate would entail costly frontal attacks. It was going to be a long war.

The United States, though, was very much at peace that fall as 2nd Lt. Dwight Eisenhower took up his duties with the 19th Infantry Regiment at Fort Sam Houston, San Antonio, Texas. One Sunday afternoon in early October, neatly attired in duty uniform—complete with polished brown boots—he was serving as officer of the guard. Standing near the officers' club, Ike was called over to a group sitting at an outside table. An Army wife acquaintance wanted him to meet her visitors. One of them was eighteen-year-old Mamie Geneva Doud, who bore a striking resemblance to the actress Lillian Gish. Mamie was there with her parents, who wintered in San Antonio each year from their home in Denver. Ike was intrigued by this personable, attractive young lady. Almost immediately he started on his first major campaign: to woo and win Mamie. By Valentine's Day 1916 they were engaged.

Trouble with Pancho Villa on the Mexican border and Germany's attacks on neutral shipping that winter put increasing pressure on the Wilson administration. One result was that the small American Army took on a wartime posture, restricting leaves to emergencies. Once Mamie accepted him, Dwight considered that marriage met this criterion, and he was able to convince higher headquarters. On July 1, 1916 — the same day that he became a first lieutenant — he married Mamie at her parents' Denver home.

With the war in Europe dominating the news that fall and winter, it was becoming clear that the United States would be involved. Germany's declaration of unrestricted submarine warfare led to a break in German-U.S. relations, and on April 6, 1917, Congress declared war. Ike, like all career officers, hoped to get into combat, but that was not to be. Among his other abilities he was an excellent trainer of troops and this led to a training assignment in September at Fort Oglethorpe, Georgia. (That same month Ike and Mamie's first son, nicknamed Icky, was born.) Eventually, he ended up at Camp Colt in Gettysburg, Pennsylvania, commanding a tank training center — which had no tanks. He did so well that he was promoted to lieutenant colonel (temporary) on his twenty-eighth birthday. Later he received a Distinguished Service Medal for his services there. But when the war ended on November 11, 1918, he was depressed, feeling that he had missed the greatest war in history.

By early 1919 the wartime Army of 2.6 million was rapidly diminishing in size; by the following year it would be down to 130,000. As the decline erased temporary promotions, Lieutenant Colonel Eisenhower found himself a major again. By March Ike was at Camp Meade, Maryland, while Mamie was in Denver. The job, demobilizing soldiers, was not especially demanding, but when something did turn up that sounded exciting, he jumped at the chance to participate.

The Army had decided to send a truck convoy from coast to coast to test its vehicles. Besides being a publicity stunt — to show Americans the kind of equipment used during the war — the trek had a more serious purpose. Though the highways up and down the eastern seaboard were adequate for that time, those going from east to west, especially across the Mississippi, were another story. Most were unpaved. The trip would dramatize the country's lack of main highways.

The convoy left Washington, D.C., on July 7 and arrived in San Francisco on September 6, averaging approximately five miles an hour. As Ike said later in his memoir, he wanted to go along "partly for a lark and partly to learn."[1] He and a friend, Maj. Serano Brett, did find the jaunt great fun, an opportunity for hunting, fishing, and playing poker and practical jokes. But the experience was also the genesis of one of his greatest presidential achievements. In his trip report, Ike recommended an effort be made to generate interest in a better highway system. Many years later, after having observed the German autobahns, he decided as president to push for what became the U.S. Interstate Highway System.[2]

On returning to Camp Meade in the fall of 1919, Ike found that some interesting changes there were offering more challenging prospects. Many senior officers of the Tank Corps in the American Expeditionary Force (AEF) were now assigned to Meade. In the four years since his West Point graduation Ike had proven to be a remarkably successful leader genuinely interested in people. He was also, though, a brilliant and ambitious young officer. Now he had an opportunity to work with combat veterans in developing his ideas on tactical doctrine for the Army of the future.

One of the veterans who interested him most was, as he later put it, "a fellow named Patton." The two West Pointers had quite different personalities. Five years older than Ike, George Patton came from a wealthy family and was an avid polo player. Eccentric in mannerisms, as well as in dress, he was inclined to be dogmatic and impatient. Still, the two had plenty in common: both were students of warfare and intensely interested in thinking about the tank's impact on future tactical doctrine. Later, both published provocative articles stressing its role. Ike, in fact, was called before the chief of infantry and told that if he published any such article in the future, incompatible with infantry doctrine, he would be court-martialed.[3]

Neighbors of the Pattons at Meade, the Eisenhowers soon became their friends, and this led to further social contacts. One Sunday afternoon in the fall of 1920 Ike and Mamie were invited to dinner at the Pattons', where the guests of honor were Gen. and Mrs. Fox Conner. Patton had known him when the general was chief of operations for Gen. John Pershing in France. In the fall of 1920 Conner was still serving his old boss, presently as his Chief of Staff for what was left of the AEF, now relocated to Washington. The dinner was a great success, and the Eisenhowers proved to be highly compatible with the Conners.

After dinner George and Ike gave the general a tour of Camp Meade, particularly featuring the tanks. They also gave their ideas on future tactics for employing this weapon. Conner was most interested, asked many questions, and encouraged them in their efforts. The general left for Washington greatly impressed with Ike's analytical approach as well as with the depth of his knowledge. This contact, as Ike later said, had a "tremendous influence" on his life.

Ike and Mamie had a happy family life at Camp Meade. They were particularly delighted with their son, Icky, an active, energetic boy who turned three in the fall of 1920. But tragedy struck. Shortly before Christmas Icky contracted scarlet fever, and on January 2 the Eisenhowers suffered a tremendous blow: Icky died. As Ike wrote nearly a half-century later, "This was the greatest disappointment and disaster in my life."[4]

A few months after Conner's visit to Meade, he sent word to Ike that he was headed to Panama to command an infantry brigade. Would Ike like to go along as his executive officer? Indeed he would. Ike's application did not get very far, though; his current superior wanted to retain him, partly because he was coaching the Meade football team. Eventually, Conner prevailed, since his close friend General Pershing was now Army Chief of Staff. Ike was ordered to report for Panama duty in January 1922.

Conner was the first of the three generals with whom Eisenhower served who greatly influenced his life. With a reputation as one of the smartest officers in the Army, Conner was particularly interested in military history, both its philosophers and its great captains. Before long he had Ike involved in a reading program that included von Clausewitz, Tacitus, the campaigns of Napoleon, and more. After each reading the two analyzed such things as reasons for the decisions and their effect upon the outcome of battles. Sometimes these talks took place in Conner's quarters but more frequently on days when they were conducting reconnaissance on horseback along the jungle trails. In essence, the two and one-half years in Panama became a graduate course for Ike, with Conner as the professor.

The general also convinced Eisenhower that because of the harsh terms of the Treaty of Versailles another European war was inevitable. Conner was joined in this view by some others such as John Maynard Keynes, who described the treaty as being "without nobility, without morality, without intellect." Conner went a step further in his discussion by stating his belief that the United States would be in the war and, further, that a unified command would be absolutely necessary. This would avoid the national bickering and uncoordinated operations that he had observed while serving in Gen. John J. Pershing's headquarters during the Great War. In later years, writing about his Panama tour and General Conner, Ike had this to say: "In a lifetime of association with great and good men, he is the one more or less invisible figure to whom I owe an incalculable debt."[5]

Beyond the professional rewards of the Panama tour, it was also a fulfilling time for Ike and Mamie, especially the summer of 1922 with the arrival of their second son, John Sheldon Doud Eisenhower. The center of Ike's life remained his family.

Conner's influence did not end with Ike's return to the States in 1924. The general, now back in Washington as deputy to the

Army Chief of Staff, arranged for him to become a student at the Army's prestigious Command and General Staff School at Fort Leavenworth, Kansas, in 1925. It was there that Eisenhower first stood out from his contemporaries. Competing with 275 of the best officers in the Army, the indifferent student of West Point days graduated first in his class. This was a major career step for Ike; he was now a young officer with a potential for going places. The problem was, where was there to go in the U.S. Army of 1926?

En route to his next assignment at Fort Benning, Georgia, he stopped in Abilene for a family reunion. An unforgettable photograph taken on the porch of the Eisenhower home shows the six boys seated with their parents, Ida and David. By then each son had his own profession: Ray, a pharmacist; Arthur, a banker; Earl, an engineer; Edgar, a lawyer; Milton, in the process of going from the consular service to the Department of Agriculture; and Ike, a thirty-six-year-old major in uniform.

The Benning assignment did not last long, for the hidden hand of Fox Conner was busy again. In 1923 Congress had established in Washington the American Battle Monuments Commission, charged with memorializing our war dead and establishing cemeteries for them in Europe. The first chairman was Gen. "Black Jack" Pershing, then retired from the Army. Pershing wanted to publish a guidebook for the American battlefields of the Great War. What he needed was someone who could bring all the related material together in a cogent manner and could write it up in an interesting fashion for the general reader. Conner had just the man. Ike got the job.

Assigned to the commission, Ike was working on the guidebook for a short time when word came that he had been selected as a student in the 1927–28 class at the nearby Army War College, the top school in the Army system. To be chosen just twelve years out of West Point was a real achievement. When the course ended, the guidebook revision was still waiting. Would Ike like to return to this project, which would entail a year in France studying the actual battlefields? Indeed he would!

The year in France was rewarding both personally and professionally. The Eisenhowers found an apartment on Quai d'Auteil near Pont Mirabeau, where they had visitors frequently. Mamie was good at entertaining, enjoyed it, and became known as a wonderful hostess. Ike's work took him to every American battlefield from Ypres to the Argonne. He had a remarkable opportunity to study the terrain, roads, and railroads of France. Inevitably, he started studying the French Army and, to a lesser extent, the country's political system. When asked years later which of his military assignments he had enjoyed most, he replied, "The year in France."

The Eisenhowers arrived back in New York from Ike's European assignment on September 24, 1929. No one could have known it then, but America was on the threshold of a new era — the Roaring Twenties with flappers dancing the Charleston, bathtub gin, and all that jazz were over. Exactly one month after Ike's return came "Black Thursday," the collapse of the Wall Street stock exchange, setting in motion a string of events leading to the Great Depression, one of the most profoundly disturbing events of the twentieth century. Its worldwide impact would eventually lead to the greatest war in human history. In that conflict Dwight Eisenhower would be a major player, but that was more than a decade in the future. For the time being Ike's new duties were in the office of the Assistant Secretary of War in Washington.

After the war those who, like Bernard Baruch, had led the mobilization of American industry in 1917–18 influenced the content of the National Defense Act of 1920. Among other things, the act stressed the importance of peacetime planning for industrial mobilization in wartime. It also created the position of assistant secretary of war with the responsibility for supervising that planning. When Ike took up his duties, the assistant secretary was Frederick Payne, a New Englander. Ike's immediate boss was Gen. George Moseley, who had managed Pershing's supply requirements in the AEF.

They confronted a basic question: How in time of war could

the U.S. economy transform from its market orientation to one focused on support of the war effort? In examining plant conversions, sources for critical raw materials, and price controls, the planners had to take into account domestic political concerns. Given this agenda, Ike found himself meeting with industrialists as well as with high government officials. He was, in fact, rounding out his previous studies of strategy and tactics with a realistic look at the logistical requirements for supporting large mechanized armies in the future. Though the work was frustrating at times, it was also intriguing, and he gained an insight into what he later called the military-industrial complex.

General Moseley turned out to be an excellent boss and at the same time a senior officer Ike felt to be a good friend. Then, about a year into the job, there came a new personality with whom Ike would be associated for nine years. Gen. Douglas MacArthur was appointed Army Chief of Staff in November 1930. Already a legend, MacArthur was working hard at expanding it. Commander of an infantry brigade in the war, he became a general at age thirty-eight. After the war he had been named superintendent at West Point; now at fifty he held the Army's highest position. MacArthur was much more interested in getting involved in planning issues than his predecessor had been. Early in his tenure, as he began looking into mobilization planning, he came in contact with Eisenhower. Impressed with Ike's writing ability MacArthur arranged for him to pen the Chief of Staff's annual report for 1931 and soon got him into matters other than writing.

Nineteen thirty-two was the cruelest year of the Depression. Unemployment was rampant, the cities had breadlines and soup kitchens, and a popular song was "Brother, Can You Spare a Dime?" The plaint of increasing numbers of AEF veterans was, "Congress, can you spare our promised bonus?" The veteran's bonus, approved by Congress in 1924, was to be payable in 1945 at the rate of one dollar for each day's war service in the United States and at $1.25 for each day's service overseas. Rep. Wright Patman of Texas had introduced legislation authorizing early payment, but it looked as if Congress might not go along. As a result, veterans throughout the country began marching on Washington. By July 1932 the Bonus Expeditionary Force (BEF), as they called themselves, numbered some fifteen thousand in the Washington area. When the Senate rejected early payment, all hell broke loose, and the district police could not handle the situation. On July 28 President Hoover ordered the Army to evict the BEF.

As to exactly what happened next, there are as many stories as there were principals involved. However, when MacArthur received the order he decided to personally lead the Army troops — who carried rifles with fixed bayonets and wore gas masks — and told Ike to get in uniform and come with him. A famous picture appeared in many newspapers: MacArthur, observing the Army troops in action, is wiping his face with a cloth. Near him, also dressed in uniform with boots, is Maj. Dwight Eisenhower smoking a cigarette. The troops with the bayonets and tear gas won, and the bonus marchers were sent packing. Reacting vehemently to the eviction, the public felt that the Hoover administration considered the heroes of 1918 to be the bums of 1932. Hoover might as well have started packing himself; the presidential election was less than four months off.

The winter of 1932–33 marked the beginning of a major change in the federal government's role as the Hoover administration gave way to Roosevelt's New Deal. It also marked the departure of Hoover's political appointees, including Frederick Payne, and Ike was transferred to MacArthur's immediate office. Here, separated from the chief only by a slatted door, he worked on reports, statements, and important letters for MacArthur's signature. He frequently discovered that the general's interests went beyond normal military matters and into political affairs. Whether he wanted to or not, Eisenhower was adding another dimension to his background.

That spring brought Roosevelt's historic "hundred days" and with it a host of new programs. One of the most important was the Civilian Conservation Corps (CCC), which became a major task for the Army. As MacArthur's assistant, Major Eisenhower became involved in preparing the chief's reports on the program. Basically, the Army was required on rather short notice to assemble and provide for approximately 200,000 previously unemployed men in small camps throughout the country. Supervised by the Departments of Agriculture and Interior, the men worked out of the camps on conservation projects. This program was to last all through the 1930s. Though it deviated in some respects from the Army's primary mission, the CCC provided many benefits over the years, including leadership training to the thousands of reserve officers who served tours as camp commanders in the 1930s.

Working directly for MacArthur entailed long hours at the office for Ike, but his personal life was a happy one. He, Mamie, and John lived in the same apartment in downtown Washington as they had back in the War College days. By now his brother Milton was director of information for Henry Wallace, secretary of commerce, and the two families were close. Other friends such as the Pattons, who lived in northern Virginia, made for a good social life. Still, as time went, the question *where from here* began to arise frequently in Ike's mind. The answer was to come in time from the other side of the slatted door.

MacArthur's tour as Chief of Staff would normally have ended in 1934, but Roosevelt extended it for another year. Since the general had become increasingly dependent on Ike's assistance, especially in composing written materials, Major Eisenhower also found his tour extended. Ike was impressed with the chief's ability to make his case convincingly before Congress, or whenever necessary, by mastering details and presenting them with logic and authority. The general was also blessed with a fast and facile mind, permitting him to respond persuasively to counterarguments.

Ike was learning a good deal from his boss, but in personality they were quite different. Though personable, MacArthur was a supreme egotist and consummate actor who routinely referred to himself in the third person. Ike remained the man from Abilene: considerate of others, enthusiastic — certainly not egotistical —

and with many warm friends. Neither two decades in the Army nor MacArthur had changed that; notwithstanding, the man from Abilene was in his own way just as ambitious as his more flamboyant chief.

As MacArthur's tour as Chief of Staff came toward its close, the general naturally began thinking of his future. Prominent in his thoughts was a country in which both he and his father had served as American proconsul — the Philippines. These islands had been acquired by the United States as a result of the Spanish-American War. By the 1930s many sectors of American society considered them a liability; hence, in 1934 Congress passed a bill granting them independence in 1946. Meanwhile, the Philippines would become semiautonomous upon installing its own government. Before he was appointed Chief of Staff, MacArthur had commanded the Army's Department of the Philippines. One of his admirers then was Manuel Quezon, who was then to head the new commonwealth. He approached MacArthur with an offer: Would he like to become the military adviser to the new nation after completing his tour as Chief of Staff? MacArthur accepted enthusiastically.

Even before Quezon had made the offer, the general had started Ike working on a preliminary plan to develop a Philippine defense force. To assist, Dwight recruited a Spanish-speaking classmate, Jimmy Ord. When they presented their plan to MacArthur, he was impressed. Obviously, Ike's role was no longer that of just a writer; his success with projects such as this one made the chief more and more dependent upon him. Not surprisingly, then, one day in the summer of 1935 a call came from the other side of the slatted door, "Major Eisenhower, I'd like to speak to you." Result: in the early fall Ike, along with Jimmy Ord, headed for Manila. Mamie and John would remain in the States for a while.

In Manila Ike served as chief of MacArthur's small staff and continued to work on the general's major problems. Becoming as well the liaison between MacArthur and Quezon, he began to develop a reputation as a good diplomat. The basic question facing the group was how to develop a defense plan that a nation of limited resources could afford. This meant a small regular force with maximum reliance on reserves. The strategy itself was defensive, designed to react to an invasion, which, of course, could come from only one country, Japan. After inflicting as much attrition as possible on the invader, the Philippine force would then fall back to a defensive area and await outside help, that is, from the United States. Implementing the defensive plan required training some thirty thousand young men each year for the reserves and obtaining the required equipment, not an easy task for a poor country.

In 1936 Mamie and John joined Ike in Manila at about the same time as his promotion to lieutenant colonel. Living in a suite at the Manila Hotel, they could look out at the bustling harbor and across the bay toward Corregidor. Life was pleasant, but the climate was hard on Mamie, and John was away most of the time at school in Baguio. Work with MacArthur was frequently a bit less pleasant, as the two did not see eye to eye on many things. Dwight, though, had tremendous respect for MacArthur. Later on, he was to say that he was deeply grateful for the experience, without which he "would not have been ready for the great responsibilities of the war." Still, their difference in temperament was wearying, and Ike felt more and more that it was time to get back into the mainstream of the Army.

Something more — much more — was pushing Ike in that direction: the international situation, particularly in Europe. Though their planning in Manila had been directed toward the threat of Japan, increasingly most Americans were focused on the relentless march of the Nazis in Europe: Rhineland 1936, Austria 1938, Munich 1938, Czechoslovakia 1939. Then, on August 23, 1939, came the bombshell: a Soviet-German pact, followed on September 1 by the invasion of Poland. On September 3, as Ike listened with earphones on a friend's antiquated radio, he heard the tired voice of British Prime Minister Neville Chamberlain. No listener would ever forget those words: "This morning the British ambassador handed the German government a note —

that unless we heard that they were prepared to withdraw from Poland, a state of war would exist. I have to tell you now that no such understanding was received and consequently this country is at war with Germany." Fox Conner had been right—the long armistice was over!

Despite pressure by MacArthur and pleas by Quezon for him to stay, Ike was determined to get back to the Army. Quezon awarded Lieutenant Colonel Eisenhower his country's Distinguished Service Cross, and when the Eisenhowers sailed on December 13, 1939, the MacArthurs (the general had married Jean Faircloth in 1937) saw them off at a stateroom party. They were in San Francisco for New Year's Eve. As dawn broke, Ike wondered what lay ahead for him in this new decade of the 1940s.

Chapter 3

General Ike

I N 1936 Franklin Roosevelt challenged the nation with these now-famous words: "This generation of Americans has a rendezvous with destiny." As 1940 began, the rendezvous was still ahead, but the clock was ticking faster. That year and the following turned out to be vital in preparing the country for the coming maelstrom. Considering events occurring in other parts of the world, the United States could characterize 1940–41 as the borrowed years. For Dwight Eisenhower they were the final phase of his apprenticeship before fate placed him on the world stage.

Ike's long-awaited troop duty turned out to be with the 15th Infantry Regiment located at Fort Lewis, Washington. Though he was a strict disciplinarian, his warm personality and sincere interest in his soldiers came through clearly. Recognizing a natural leader, the troops respected and liked him. Being at Fort Lewis, just south of Tacoma, where Ike's brother Edgar had his law practice, the Eisenhowers were able to have close contact with Edgar and his family. This would be John's last year at home, since, while still in the Philippines, he had decided that he wanted to attend West Point. By the fall of 1940 he was off to a Washington,

D.C., prep school to prepare for the competitive exam. Because Abilene was still Dwight's legal residence, the exam was given by a senator from Kansas.

The Army that Ike returned to in 1940 numbered about 240,000, but events that spring, particularly in Europe, demanded a major expansion and a change in tempo. After German and Soviet forces had overrun Poland the previous September, the lull in military action prompted public references to the "phony war" or "sitzkrieg." In April, though, the designation was changed to blitzkrieg when Hitler's forces overran Denmark and most of Norway in short order. Beginning May 10 came Hitler's campaign in the West, one of the world's great military masterpieces: Holland and Belgium overrun; the British and some Allies evacuated from Dunkirk; then on June 22, France surrendered. Even before that date, pictures in newspapers showing German troops parading past the Arc de Triomphe in Paris signaled to the rest of the world that the lights were going out in Western Europe.

Wasting no time, FDR went before Congress on May 16 to call for large-scale rearmament of the United States. As events unfolded in Europe, he met an increasingly responsive public and Congress. Perhaps the most difficult of the steps to get through Congress was the Selective Service Bill, which he signed on September 16; it required the registration for military service of all males twenty-one to thirty-five. By the end of October came the draft lottery itself with the initial goal of an Army of 1.5 million.

During the spring of 1940 the Third Infantry Division, to which the 15th was assigned, conducted maneuvers south of Monterey, California. It marked the beginning of an expanding army that was also absorbing and training with new equipment, such as tanks and the 81-mm mortar. An even more important goal was to develop the junior leaders who would soon be responsible for training the new draftees. Ike was in his element, eighteen-hour days, working with his "youngsters," and watching them develop into soldiers. These would be the young men on whom so much would depend so soon.

By summer the maneuvers had been raised to corps level back in Washington State just south of Fort Lewis. The division commander, Maj. Gen. Charles Thompson, had kept his eye on Ike through both of these maneuvers, and in November he made his move. Ike was great with troops, but Thompson needed an experienced Chief of Staff who could coordinate the expansion that would come as new draftees arrived. Like it or not, Dwight was back to staff duty in November, this time as Chief of Staff of the Third "Rock of the Marne" Division.

In the winter of 1940–41, as the new draftees poured in, came a multitude of problems: receiving, housing, and caring for the troops and, most important, training them. Maneuvers were finished for a while; now it was small-unit training again. By late winter, when the training moved up a notch to larger units, so would Ike. The IX Corps, also based at Lewis, was charged with supervising the training of Army units in northwestern United States. Its commander, Maj. Gen. Kenyon Joyce, formerly with the Third Division, needed a new Chief of Staff. He got his choice, Eisenhower. On March 11 the general pinned the eagles of a full colonel on Ike's collar. In peacetime that was the top rank for all but a few, but now the bets at Lewis were that it would not be long before Dwight Eisenhower pinned on a star.

Though fully engaged in his various positions in the Lewis days, Ike tried to keep himself informed on events in Europe. The summer of 1940 saw the Battle of Britain, when Churchill declared of the Royal Air Force, "Never in the field of human conflict was so much owed by so many to so few." On September 15 the German air raids reached their peak, but their losses were staggering. The RAF downed fifty-six Luftwaffe planes in one forty-five-minute period alone. Though the raids continued, mainly in an attempt to destroy British morale — St. Paul's Cathedral October 10, Coventry November 14 — the German radio stopped playing "We Sail against England." The British Isles would soon serve as a potential base for the strike against Hitler's Germany whenever and however that would come.

Among the many war-connected events that winter, a dispatch

about a new German initiative caught Dwight's eye. On February 14 a German force called the Afrika Korps had arrived in Libya with the goal of reversing the setbacks that the British were administering to the Italian forces. The dispatch mentioned that the commander of the Afrika Korps was a German general named Erwin Rommel.

In Washington, meanwhile, the high command of the Army had plans under way for a huge maneuver designed to train and test Army commanders and staffs in handling large troop formations in a simulated wartime situation. George Marshall, Army chief since September 1939, and Lt. Gen. Leslie J. McNair, the chief planner, had decided to pit two armies against each other in Louisiana. On one side would be the Second Army with a force of about 180,000 troops commanded by Lt. Gen. Ben (or, according to the draftees, "Yoo Hoo") Lear. On the other side, the Third Army with a force of 240,000 troops would be commanded by Lt. Gen. Walter Krueger. The Third was based at Fort Sam Houston in San Antonio, where Krueger needed a Chief of Staff capable of managing the tactical and logistical complexities in maneuvering a force of that size against an "enemy." After McNair studied the possible choices, the order came through: Col. Dwight Eisenhower was to report to Third Army in late June 1941 to serve as Chief of Staff.

Although San Antonio was a homecoming of sorts, especially for Mamie, there were differences. They now lived in a large house with high ceilings rather than in a converted bachelor's apartment — and had an enlisted orderly to boot! Ike had little time at home, though. Along with his deputy, Lieutenant Colonel Gruenther, he was deeply involved in planning for the great maneuver. In early August General Krueger, a hands-on type of commander, moved his entire army into Louisiana for some preliminary training — and a good thing, too. The citizen soldiers needed plenty of work to blend them into effective combat units, but by the 13th of September Krueger and Ike thought they were ready to take on the Second Army.

The first phase, which began on September 15, had the Third

Army advancing up the Mississippi, while Lear's Second Army was given the objective of pushing them back into the Gulf of Mexico. Chief of Staff Ike was in his element, with Conner's years of tutorials and his own hard work now paying off. The first phase ended after four days with a victory for Krueger's army. For the first time Ike received national newspaper coverage. An article by Drew Pearson and Robert Allen described him as having "a steel trap mind and unusual physical vigor."[1] The second phase began on the 24th with Lear in the attack; next day the tables were turned, and the Third Army began a successful counterattack. It was all over by the 27th. Again the press gave much of the credit to Eisenhower. The reporters liked this approachable colonel who could explain in clear terms what was happening during the maneuver.

When the critique of the maneuver ended, Generals Marshall and McNair made a point of meeting Ike, whose performance at the maneuvers had caused Krueger to recommend him for promotion. Two days later he was promoted to brigadier general. After the return to Fort Sam the immediate task was to get the maneuver's lessons out to the troop units for incorporation into their training programs. The months of October and November sped by as Ike continued putting in long days.

Earlier that summer Hitler had begun his most daring adventure: operation Barbarossa, the German invasion of Russia. Without a declaration of war he initiated the greatest land battle in recorded history across a thousand-mile front. At first the German forces seemed unstoppable; as the weeks went by, an increasingly tenacious Russian defense along with the sheer magnitude of the supply and support problem began to take its toll. Then came an early Russian winter, which turned out to be the harshest one in half a century. Hitler's forces were not ready for it, and on December 6 the Soviet forces launched their counterattack. The only Germans who made it to Moscow were prisoners of war.

But now American public attention had a new focus, shifting from Europe to Asia, where Japan was becoming increasingly aggressive in both rhetoric and action. The Japanese had long wanted to be the overseers of Asia and the western Pacific, and to control the raw materials and trade of the area under the rubric of the "Greater East Asia Co-Prosperity Sphere." The United States had striven for many years against that policy. Now in the fall of 1941 the Japanese were pushing for an end to American aid to China, as well as removal of the embargo on shipments of scrap iron and gasoline that Roosevelt had placed on them in July 1941. By December, the situation had become tense and Roosevelt dispatched an urgent personal note to the Japanese emperor pleading for a peaceful settlement.

On the first Sunday in December Ike worked all morning in his office, trying to clear up a backlog of staff actions. He and Mamie were looking forward to a holiday, when they could visit John, a plebe at West Point. At noon Dwight headed home for a nap, asking Mamie not to disturb him. An hour later the phone at his bedside rang; he was on his feet in an instant. The Japanese were attacking Pearl Harbor. Five days later he received a call from Col. Walter Bedell Smith, who worked directly for General Marshall. "The chief says for you to get up here right away."

When Ike swung down from the train at Washington's Union Station on Sunday morning, December 14, he entered a city in turmoil and transition. One week after Pearl Harbor the capital was a magnet, drawing in experts from many fields to help direct the nation's efforts. The conflict was now global, Germany and Italy having declared war on the United States on December 11, with the United States reciprocating. Few of the new arrivals, however, were at their jobs as quickly as General Eisenhower. That same morning he found himself seated in front of the cool customer who had summoned him to Washington — George Catlett Marshall, Army Chief of Staff since 1939. Ike had seen Marshall only briefly on three previous occasions. Now the general was giving him an outline of the situation in the Pacific. After about twenty minutes the chief stopped to ask, "What should be our general course of action?" Requesting a few hours to think it over, his new plans officer was off and running.

The most immediate problem area for the War and Navy Departments was the Pacific, particularly what, if anything, could be done to save the Philippines, which the Japanese had invaded a few days after the Pearl Harbor attack. As the principal Pacific planner for Marshall, Ike worked long hours on the problem, along with many other staff officers and agencies. In the end, though, Bataan fell in April and Corregidor in May. MacArthur, meanwhile, had been evacuated to Australia. There his mission was to establish a base for launching a Pacific offensive when the time came.

In the late 1930s American planners had concluded that, if we were faced with a global war, the best American strategy at the outset would be to adopt a defensive role in the Pacific and to mount the main effort in Europe. By 1941 this concept also coincided with the best interests of Great Britain and the Soviet Union, already heavily engaged with the Nazis. Taking advantage of Allied efforts already under way, this strategy would also be in the best interests of the United States. As the winter wore on, Ike's planning focused on the European region and even more so in early March, when Marshall appointed him as the first chief of the newly established Operations Division, which became Marshall's command post during World War II. A couple of days later Eisenhower pinned on the stars of a major general — his third promotion in a year!

Ike's brother Milton had been in Washington for about sixteen years. Though ostensibly handling public information for the Department of Agriculture, he frequently took on special projects for the secretary and occasionally for the White House. Milton, his wife, Helen, and their two youngsters were able to provide Ike a home environment as he awaited Mamie's arrival in early February. Anticipating their being in Washington for the duration, Mamie brought their furniture along, and after a short hotel stay the Eisenhowers moved into quarters at Fort Myer, Virginia.

During the six months that Ike had daily contact with George Marshall, the chief became the third of the three senior officers who greatly influenced his career. Marshall was totally different in personality and outlook from the flamboyant MacArthur. Without grandiose pronouncements or public posturing, Marshall proved just as persuasive in argument. Quiet and modest, he had a most successful relationship with the media, the other services, and President Roosevelt. In short, he was for Ike an ideal example of a superb leader at the highest level of political-military decision making.

It was one thing to agree on a Germany-first concept and another to come up with a realistic offensive strategy. What was clear, though, was whatever the nature of this offensive, the British Isles would be the launching base and, hence, the location of the supporting logistical buildup. Ike and his colleagues were busy on such a support plan, code-named Bolero. Simultaneously, he was preparing the assault plan itself, called Roundup, with a tentative starting date of April 1943. The plans division also developed a contingency plan — which horrified the British — to launch an assault against the Continent in September 1942 in case either the Soviet Union or the Nazis began to collapse.[2]

On the 1st of April Ike and his team presented their planning concepts to Marshall. After long discussion Marshall approved these and took them to FDR for his approval. The President agreed, subject to securing British concurrence, which everyone considered absolutely essential. The President dispatched his personal assistant, Harry Hopkins, to accompany Marshall to London for a meeting of the minds with the British. The emissaries met with Churchill and the top British officers, but the best they could get was an agreement "in principle." Churchill was wary of a direct assault on the Continent. What intrigued him was an invasion of what he called the "soft underbelly" of Europe after securing a base in North Africa. The agreement "in principle" was enough for Marshall. American planning would continue to be based on a direct assault of the continent from Britain. Whatever operations were undertaken in the Mediterranean would be preliminary to the main invasion.

While debriefing Eisenhower on the trip's results, Marshall

expressed his doubts about whether the American headquarters in London — established before Pearl Harbor — could handle the major problems lying ahead. Pershing's difficult experiences with the Allies during the AEF days had impressed Marshall with the absolute need for close Allied cooperation at the highest levels. He asked Ike to go to Britain, take a look, and come up with his recommendations for a new American headquarters. No doubt Marshall had still another thought in the back of his mind: that this trip would give the British an excellent opportunity to look over Dwight Eisenhower.

During his week in Britain Ike spent enough time with the senior American personnel to be convinced that the existing organization was inadequate for the task ahead. He also met with many of the senior British leaders, beginning with Winston Churchill. At a meeting with Chief of the Imperial General Staff Alan Brooke there was some inconclusive sparring on the issue of command arrangements for Roundup. Ike was particularly impressed with two senior British officers: Gen. Bernard Law Montgomery and the youthful Lord Louis Mountbatten, who was involved with developing doctrine and techniques for assault landings on a hostile shore. By the time Ike returned to Washington, word had reached Marshall that his planner was a great hit with the British.

On June 8 Eisenhower briefed Marshall on a proposed organization and mission for a European Theater of Operations. Leaving the proposal with the chief, Ike suggested that he read it carefully. After indicating that he would indeed, Marshall looked straight at Ike and said, "You may be the man who executes it. If so, when can you leave?" Three days later he told Ike to start packing. On Monday morning, June 22, Ike said good-bye to Mamie and headed out to Bolling Field, pondering the enormous task ahead, along with Marshall's last words to him, "You go over and do a good job."[3]

The day after his arrival in London, Eisenhower, commander of the newly established U.S. European Theater of Operations, held his first press conference. From that point on, he became a world figure, his meetings with the press normally rating a front-page story. With the media Ike was a natural: relaxed, friendly, straightforward, and looking every bit a soldier. Well aware of the importance of the press in molding public opinion, he became very skilled in using it on behalf of the Allied cause.

Essential to that cause was Anglo-American unity; Ike stressed it constantly with his own staff and subordinate commanders. He also worked hard at it himself in his contacts with the British press, public, and leadership, both political and military. Among the military one personality was not susceptible to Eisenhower's charm — Bernard "Monty" Montgomery.

Ike's daily routine was a continuous round of meetings, conferences, visits with troop units, and social events that he was unable to avoid. Understandably, he felt the need for a place outside of London, at least for weekends, that he could call home. The solution came in August with the rental of a small house in Surrey known as Telegraph Cottage. Equally important to him was to feel at home with his immediate entourage, in time known as the "Eisenhower family." Best known of the eight making up that group were Henry Butcher, a wartime Navy officer and friend since the late 1920s who served as Eisenhower's naval aide; Maj. Tex Lee, his Army aide; Sgt. Mickey McKeough, his enlisted orderly, with him since the San Antonio period the previous year; and Kay Summersby, his driver, then a member of the British Motor Transport Corps.

At the official level Ike wanted a tough Chief of Staff, and he got one in Brig. Gen. Walter Bedell Smith, after convincing Marshall to release "Beetle" from Washington. With him on board the two of them worked together to get results by employing the good-guy, bad-guy routine, Ike of course being the good guy.

In that summer of 1942 Eisenhower exuded optimism, even though operations left little to be optimistic about on the Russian front or in North Africa. German forces were on the Don, ready to push toward Stalingrad. In North Africa Rommel was on the move again and by late June had pushed across the Egyptian frontier to El Alamein. The Afrika Korps posed a potential threat to the Suez Canal. It was in the light of these events that major strategic decision making took place in July.

No question that both Marshall and Eisenhower were committed to the concept that a cross-channel invasion of Europe was necessary if the Nazi forces were to be destroyed. The earliest such an operation could take place would be 1943 and then only after a dedicated buildup in Britain of American units and logistical support. Meanwhile, both generals became increasingly aware of several political and military realities that presaged a 1942 operation, probably in North Africa. Included were these pressing concerns:

1. Russian demands that something be done to take German pressure off the eastern front.
2. The need to reopen British shipping lanes in the Mediterranean. This would require destroying German forces in North Africa.
3. Roosevelt's anticipation of increasing home-front pressure to take some offensive action with American forces in this year of congressional elections. After all, it had been two years since the draft began.
4. The need for American armed forces to gain battle experience before engaging in the invasion of Europe.

All these considerations coalesced in July when Marshall, Hopkins, and a large entourage of officers came to London to reach strategic decisions with the British. The concept of an emergency cross-channel operation in 1942, partly to assuage the Soviets, met outright rejection by Churchill and his associates. (The disastrous outcome of the August Dieppe raid, conducted by the British largely with Canadian forces, was to confirm the soundness of Churchill's decision.) In the end Roosevelt agreed with the British that an operation into North Africa in the fall of 1942 would be the way to go. July 24 saw the final decision: North Africa was to be invaded, and Lt. Gen. Dwight Eisenhower would command the operation.

Established by November 5 in his Gibraltar operations center under eighteen feet of solid rock, Ike awaited the initiation of the Allied invasion of North Africa (Operation Torch) on the 8th. Though the major operational decisions had been made in England, Ike still had a political-military problem to confront the day before the invasion. French Gen. Henri Giraud, formerly a German prisoner, had been spirited out of France as a potential non-Vichy symbol of his country; on the eve of the invasion he met with Eisenhower. Ike's goal was to persuade Giraud to use his alleged prestige to convince the French North African forces to support, rather than oppose, the Allied landings. After hours of discussion all Ike received initially from Giraud was Gallic posturing, leading nowhere.

Three task forces were employed in the Torch landings. The western force, entirely American and commanded by Maj. Gen. George Patton, sailed directly from the United States, landing on the Atlantic coast in the Casablanca vicinity. The center, also American, came from the British Isles under command of Maj. Gen. Lloyd Fredendall and had Oran as its objective. The eastern, landing at Algiers, also sailed from the British Isles and was composed of American and British troops commanded by Lt. Gen. Kenneth Anderson of the British Army.

Meanwhile in Egypt, the British Eighth Army, which had been rebuilt and reequipped, had been assigned a new commander, Gen. Bernard Montgomery. On October 23 he had launched a major offensive against the forces of the Desert Fox. After ten days of hammering, the British broke through and Rommel began to retreat. The British pursued deliberately but relentlessly; by the time of the Torch launching, they had almost crossed the Egyptian border into Libya with every intention of an eventual linkup with Eisenhower's forces.

Almost all the operational reports that trickled into Ike on November 8–9 were good; by the 10th, Oran and Algiers were essentially in Allied hands. Patton still had some fighting on his hands in Casablanca, and Ike, anxious to move his forces east toward Tunis, could not resist a message to him: "Crack it open quickly." Then, keeping in mind Patton's personality, he commented in humor on the office copy of the message, "Will he burn?" Meanwhile, Giraud had finally agreed to make a radio broadcast to the French forces, but they, in turn, totally ignored it. An alternative to the French general turned up unexpectedly in the person of Adm. François Darlan, second only to Gen. Philippe Pétain in the Vichy governmental hierarchy. He had been captured by chance at Algiers, where he was visiting an ailing son. Perhaps a message from him to the French forces would do the trick. Eventually, Darlan did issue a cease-fire order, but by then the Allies had already accomplished their immediate objectives. What the "Darlan Deal," as the press called it, did do was to cause Ike endless problems.

To begin with, Darlan was a fascist and an anti-Semite. What Ike had in mind in dealing with the admiral was to employ him as a symbol of French authority; for example, to gain French support in seizing the ports of Bizerte and Tunis, thus hindering German resupply and reinforcement. Perhaps the Allies might also secure the services of the French fleet, then in southern France. Actually, they achieved neither objective. By the time the Darlan deal was consummated, the Germans had already poured heavy air and ground reinforcements into Tunisia, and the capture of the two ports was going to be a long, tough battle. Later in the month the French Navy scuttled its own ships to prevent their seizure by the Germans.

What Ike did get from his first foray into political decision making was considerable criticism from the British and American press for dealing with a fascist. His brother Milton, then with the Office of War Information, was dispatched to Ike's headquarters in Algiers to help repair his public image. In a bizarre twist Darlan was assassinated on Christmas Eve by a student acting for the French Resistance. He was succeeded by Giraud as High Commissioner of French Africa.

By January the campaign had become a holding action for Eisenhower's forces. With torrential rains turning the area into a quagmire, the immediate problem was to prevent the expansion of the German bridgehead. From the east Rommel's Afrika Korps was retreating toward Tunisia pursued by Montgomery in what the Berlin radio broadcast described as a "westward advance." Meanwhile, the Soviet forces, who had launched a major offensive of their own in November, had surrounded the German Sixth Army at Stalingrad. By January 1943, despite German efforts to extricate them, their surrender was inevitable.

In mid-January Roosevelt and Churchill held one of their more famous summits at Casablanca with the Combined (British and American) Chiefs of Staff in attendance. In briefing the group on operations since November, Ike felt a bit uneasy that no one congratulated him on Torch. He did tell Marshall that his North African experience convinced him that there was no way of meeting all the logistical requirements, such as enough landing craft, to support a cross-channel operation in 1943. The British wanted to continue the campaign in the Mediterranean anyway, while Roosevelt was adamant that American troops must be in combat against German forces somewhere.

The summit's outcome was the decision to invade Sicily after completing operations in North Africa. Ike was confirmed as commander, this time assisted by three British deputies: Gen. Harold Alexander (Army); Adm. Andrew Cunningham (Navy); and Air Marshal Arthur Tedder (Air). Though all three ranked higher than Eisenhower, that was soon remedied when on February 10 Ike received his fourth star, joining only two others on active duty in the Army at that rank—Marshall and MacArthur.

By February German forces in North Africa were confined to the coastal area of Tunisia: Von Arnim's Fifth Panzer Army in the north, and digging in to the south near Mareth, Rommel's Afrika Korps. On February 14 the Germans opened an assault to buy time and to shake the Allies—about all they could hope to achieve at that point. In five days Rommel's forces penetrated deeply into the American sector through a pass named Kasserine, in the process knocking out American tanks, artillery pieces, and more. But at that point they ran out of steam and soon fell back to their original line.

As World War II combat went, the battle of Kasserine Pass was minor, but it was the baptism of fire for American forces and for Eisenhower. It had not gone well for either. The Germans had inflicted more than six thousand casualties on the Americans at a cost of about a thousand to themselves. It was, however, the last German offensive action in North Africa. Afterward, Ike reported to Marshall that American combat forces needed more realistic training, and he would see that they got it. Realizing, too, that he must be tougher in weeding out inadequate leaders, he started by firing the overall American commander at Kasserine, Gen. Lloyd Fredendall, replacing him with George Patton.

In March, after the British had repulsed another German attack, Eisenhower renewed the offensive. American forces attacked east in coordination with Montgomery's troops from the south, and on April 7 the two forces met. From then on, it was a matter of squeezing the German forces into a tighter and tighter pocket in northern Tunisia. Meanwhile, Rommel had returned to Germany ill and left Von Arnim to pay the bills. The final Allied attack began on April 22 and by May 7 the Americans entered Bizerte, and the British captured Tunis. Six days later it was over, with the enemy surrendering more than a quarter of a million troops.[4]

So ended Dwight Eisenhower's first and, in some ways, most difficult campaign. He had faced many frustrations: needing to make political decisions on matters beyond his control; confronting logistical problems on a major scale; and, above all, dealing with the inexperience of American troops. Nevertheless, the alliance that he had played a primary role in forging had wrested a continent from a determined and capable enemy. This was not the end of the enormous problems Ike would face in the war against the Axis, nor was it even the beginning of the end, but it was, to borrow a famous quotation of Churchill's, "the end of the beginning."

Chapter 4

The Great Crusade

BY JULY Eisenhower's forces were ready for Operation Husky, the invasion of Sicily. Their objective, the port of Messina in the northeast corner of the island, was just three miles from the Italian mainland. Strategically, a success would not only make Italy vulnerable to Allied assault but would also provide additional protection for Allied shipping in the Mediterranean.

Enemy forces on the island were estimated at eight divisions: six Italian and two German. Under Ike's overall command, General Alexander, 15th Army Group commander, would employ Montgomery's British Eighth Army and George Patton's American Seventh. Since spring Ike had been working out operational plans with the commanders — not an easy matter considering Monty's prickly personality. At one point he had derided an early version of the plan as "a dog's breakfast."[1] The final version had Montgomery's forces landing on the southeast coast of the island and pushing up the east coast to Messina. Patton's army would land west of them defending Monty's left flank.

On July 8 Eisenhower established his command post on Malta and on the 10th the greatest armada of the war, almost half a million Allied troops, began landing. A counterattack by the German forces under Field Marshal "Smiling Albert" Kesserling came the next day but was beaten back. Montgomery's forces pushed slowly — very slowly, some felt — up the east coast of Sicily; at the same time Patton headed for Palermo on the western tip of the island and then along the northern coast toward Messina.

When American and British troops entered Messina on August 17, the Germans were gone. Despite Allied sea and air superiority they had evacuated more than 100,000 troops to mainland Italy. Still, their casualties numbered more than 150,000, including 32,000 Germans. Afterward, Ike realized that he had been too cautious, as he felt he had been in the early stages of Torch. In hindsight he perceived that it would have been better, considering Allied air and naval superiority, to have conducted the initial assault at Messina, thus cutting off the entire enemy force. As it was, the German divisions lived to fight another day, one that was not too far off.

During his frequent visits with Ike, Churchill constantly pushed the idea of invading the Italian mainland after Sicily. Shortly after the start of the Sicily assault, the Combined Chiefs had joined him in urging Ike to consider a landing on the Italian mainland. Ike agreed but, after studying German troop deployments, decided on a prudent approach, basically beginning at the "toe" of Italy.

Meanwhile, dramatic developments, favorable to the Allies, were occurring on the Italian political scene. On July 25 Mussolini was deposed, arrested, and replaced by Marshal Pietro Badoglio, who wanted Italy out of the war but feared the Germans. What Badoglio did not know was that the Germans were well aware of what he was up to but had not yet decided where they wanted to hold the line in Italy. After agreeing secretly to an armistice, Badoglio wavered. On September 8, furious, Ike sent him a message that as Allied commander he intended to broadcast an armistice that day and expected the marshal to do his part! Going on the air, Ike announced the unconditional surrender of the Italian armed forces, and later that day Badoglio gave in with an order ending all Italian military operations. Ike was jubilant, "One down — two to go," he announced to his immediate staff.[2]

Meanwhile, Ike planned and prepared for the invasion of mainland Italy, still held by the Germans, who had pushed the Italians aside. On September 3, against little resistance, Montgomery put portions of the British Eighth Army into Italy from Messina. On September 9 the equivalent of four divisions of the American Fifth Army, commanded by Gen. Mark Clark, began going ashore farther north at Salerno just south of Naples. Expecting this hazardous operation, the enemy responded with massive counterattacks that made the beachhead extremely dangerous; at times the Germans threatened to wipe out the American force. Overcoming the threat, the Americans and British held and expanded the beachhead, coming ashore with reinforcements and supplies; by the 15th they were secure and forcing their way inland.

A week later Eisenhower ordered Alexander to continue the attack with the goal of capturing Rome — an overly optimistic objective, as it turned out. Kesserling had other ideas. He thought he could hold on between Naples (which the Allies captured in early October) and Rome. When Hitler accepted that view, Smiling Albert went about building successive defense positions, usually behind rivers, across the Italian peninsula. Though famous for their great success with the blitzkrieg in Western Europe in 1940, the Germans were also very good at this kind of warfare. By year's end the Allied forces were worn down from fighting at the successive positions, and they were still a long way from the Eternal City.

At Teheran, in late November, came the first meeting of Roosevelt and Churchill with Stalin. One agenda item discussed in great detail was the opening of the second front, Operation Overlord. Roosevelt and Churchill wanted Stalin's agreement to start a major offensive against the Germans at the same time. Stalin was wary — Soviet officials had always doubted that such an Allied invasion would take place. Who, Stalin wanted to know, would be the commander? FDR promised to let him know soon.

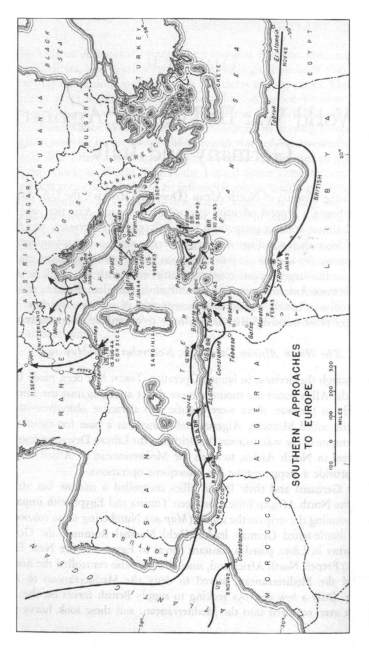

Allied Operations in the Mediterranean and Southern Europe, 1942–1945.

Afterward, the president met with Marshall to determine his personal wishes on who should command. Marshall deferred to the commander in chief. FDR said he would not be able to sleep well with Marshall out of Washington. En route home on December 6, FDR stopped off at Tunis and was met by Eisenhower. No sooner had Ike sat down next to the President in the car when in his patrician manner FDR said, "Well, Ike, you are going to command Overlord."

December became an especially busy time for Ike—still the Mediterranean commander, but now also designated Supreme Commander for the spring invasion of Europe. Shortly after FDR's departure Ike had a pneumonia-ridden Churchill on his hands. As soon as the prime minister's recovery was under way, he began pushing Ike to agree on an assault landing in Italy, this time behind the German lines at Anzio. The goal—to break the stalemate that had descended on the Italian front—was not a new idea, having been explored for many months under the code name Shingle. Its feasibility depended on resources, especially landing craft, that could be made available to the Mediterranean theater, now in direct competition with the Overlord buildup. Churchill, who could not resist playing tactician, was adamant, and with Roosevelt's concurrence the Anzio operation was scheduled for January.

To command the assault phase of Overlord and to lead the British forces later, Eisenhower wanted Alexander. He definitely did not want Montgomery, whom he found difficult to handle, and whose performance in Sicily and Italy he considered plodding. Since the defeat of Rommel, though, Monty had become a hero to the British press and public and, as it was Churchill's decision, Monty became Ike's senior ground commander for the Overlord invasion.

Also of concern to Ike that December was a different kind of Overlord problem: securing the support of the French underground prior to and during the invasion. Gen. Charles de Gaulle, who by then had pushed Giraud to the sidelines, had become the symbol and de facto leader of the Free French. On December 30

Eisenhower paid a call on "Charles le Grand" and, at least for the moment, accomplished the mission of gaining his support. Among other gestures made during this "love fest" (as Ike's naval aide Harry Butcher called it) was the Supreme Commander's agreement that the first Allied troops to enter Paris would be French. As Eisenhower soon became aware, Roosevelt and some others in Washington were reluctant to accept de Gaulle as the French leader, but they were not faced with the Supreme Commander's problems.

From Washington, Chief of Staff George Marshall pressed Ike to return home for a brief respite between his Mediterranean and Overlord responsibilities. Although reluctant, he gave in after a December 29 message from Marshall with this clincher: "Now come on home and see your wife and trust somebody else for twenty minutes in England."[3] Accompanied by Harry Butcher, he arrived in Washington in the early morning hours of January 2, 1944. The two were greeted by their wives in the hall of the Wardman Park Hotel annex, where Mamie and Ruth had apartments facing each other.

During twelve busy days in the States, Ike's visit was concealed as much as possible for a variety of reasons, but mainly to keep the Nazis off balance about the imminence of the invasion. His schedule included meetings with Marshall and other Pentagon officials, conferences with congressional leaders, and three meetings with FDR. At two of these meetings Ike raised the question of de Gaulle, pointing out his potential value in assuring the support of the French Resistance. He got nowhere with the President, for FDR had nothing but disdain for the French leader.[4]

On the personal side Ike was able to spend some time with Mamie in a cottage at White Sulphur Springs, West Virginia, and he met John at West Point in a private railroad car. Best of all was a flight back to Kansas for a brief family reunion of sorts at the home of his brother Milton, recently installed as president of Kansas State University. Brothers Edgar and Arthur were there also, as was Ida, his eighty-one-year-old mother, who greeted him with tears and laughter, "Why, it's Dwight!"

The Ike of January 1944 was quite different from the man who had left home in June 1942. Of necessity he exuded the personality of the man in charge: confident, direct, impatient, and assertive. After all, he had directed and triumphed in two major campaigns against the Axis. During the visit to the States his mind was understandably on the vast responsibilities lying ahead, along with a natural urge to want to get on with it. On January 13 as the C54 sped him toward Europe and those responsibilities, he remembered Mamie's final words to him: "Don't come back till it's over, Ike. I can't stand losing you again."[5]

Back in London Ike plunged into a series of Overlord problems that required his decision or intervention. Generally, these were matters of strategy, operational planning, command, and control of forces, or logistics. Many issues needed his talents to reconcile and smooth out differences of opinion between services or between the two principal nations — or both. As it turned out, he would have 143 days to get ready for the invasion, and he needed all of them to fit in the constant round of meetings, conferences, and visits to troop units.

The most immediate problem was to obtain the approval of the Combined Chiefs of Staff for an expanded assault force: five divisions instead of three, with a beach front of fifty, rather than thirty-five, miles. As this would entail almost three hundred more landing ships, that was indeed a problem, as they were in short supply. The Navy also needed landing ships for its drive across the central Pacific, as did MacArthur's current advance along the northern edge of New Guinea. After much wrangling, Eisenhower's problem was solved by postponing D-Day for Overlord from May to June, providing another month for LST production; scrounging up some craft from the American and British Navies; and, most controversial, postponing the planned invasion of southern France (Anvil) from D-Day until August 15.

Meanwhile, Ike faced another major issue: he wanted control of the RAF Bomber Command and the U. S. Army Air Forces, both of which were conducting strategic bombing campaigns deep inside Germany under direction of the Combined Chiefs.

What the Supreme Commander had in mind for the bombers was to conduct a prolonged and intensive destruction of French railways and bridges; in effect, to isolate the battlefield and thus prevent the Germans from moving in reinforcements when the invasion came. The debate over the Transportation Plan, as this concept was called, dragged on through February and March. Finally, Ike lost his cool, threatening to tell Churchill "to get someone else to run the war." Eisenhower finally got what he wanted, and it paid off. Unleashed, the Transportation Plan proved effective in the Normandy area and was also employed in the Pas de Calais area to the north as a diversion. It was there that the Germans really expected the invasion to come, so this part of the deception plan was aimed at keeping Nazi units pinned down, waiting there for the invasion.

A responsibility that Ike had in common with his commanders was to know the troops and to gain their confidence. One important way to accomplish this was through frequent visits and inspections, which gave him an opportunity for mingling and talking with the troops, while listening to what they had to say. Ike was particularly effective in achieving rapport with his men. By using his private railroad car, Bayonet, he was able to visit twenty-six American and British divisions, and almost the same number of air fields, along with many ships, hospitals, and the like. In time the troops felt that they knew Ike and during his visits were constantly bombarding him for his autograph.

There was one problem that the Supreme Commander was not able to resolve by D-Day: the Roosevelt-de Gaulle standoff. By that time the provisional president of France, the general wanted his country to be accepted again in its role as a great power on a level with the United States and Britain. Roosevelt, however, was of a different mind; he wanted no action by anyone, including Eisenhower, that might constitute recognition of de Gaulle and his group as the government of France. Supreme Headquarters Allied Expeditionary Forces (SHAEF) was in the middle. Ike was keenly aware that the Resistance—which accepted de Gaulle as its leader—planned to impede Nazi communication, including the disruption of the French railway system. The Supreme Commander needed its help. For the moment, though, he could do no more; any rapprochement between SHAEF and the provisional government would have to await developments during Overlord itself.

On May 15 Eisenhower met with 150 of his senior commanders and staff officers at Montgomery's old school, St. Paul's, in West Kensington for a final review of Overlord. The principal briefer was Monty, ground commander for the invasion, who moved about near a huge relief map of France that displayed Allied phase lines from D-Day to D+90, by which point the goal was to be on the River Seine. Monty began with his estimate of the enemy situation: Rommel had sixty divisions in France, of which ten were panzers, and of these perhaps six were in the Normandy area, one of which was a panzer. No doubt Rommel would try to delay the Allies on the beaches and then counterattack in an attempt to drive them back into the sea before SHAEF could build up its forces.

Turning to the Allied situation, Montgomery was optimistic. He had no doubts about holding the beaches; in fact, he expected his forces to move ahead rapidly on the first day and "peg claims well inland." There were other speakers as well, most notably the British King and Churchill. Ike, who had opened the meeting in the morning, also made the final remarks in late afternoon. Hands on hips and wearing his Ike jacket he stood in front of the impressive gathering, ending with on-to-victory remarks. Two days later he passed on to the commanders who had attended this conference an important bit of information: D-Day would be June 5.

Having completed their training, the assault troops began to move in a steady stream toward their encampments on the southern coast, after which they were sealed off from the rest of England. On June 1 Ike moved his advance command post a few miles north of Portsmouth, not far from Southwick House, where the final decision to invade would be made. This was a decision awaited not only by the Allies and the enemy, but also by the world. In the meantime the Germans had their hands full elsewhere. The U.S. Fifth Army had finally broken out of the Anzio beachhead and linked up with Alexander's main forces, now headed for Rome. On the eastern front the Soviets were assembling a huge force for a major attack, which, when it came on June 22, was to send Nazis reeling back some 250 miles in twenty-five days.

Beginning with his first meeting at Southwick House, Ike's chief concern was one over which he had no control but was of central importance to the invasion's success — the weather. The chief meteorologist, Group Captain Stagg, warned that the weather developing over Iceland and heading toward the invasion area might be bad news, but only time would tell. Meanwhile, Ike wrote his Order of the Day for the invasion beginning: "Soldiers, sailors, and airmen of the Allied Expeditionary Force: You are about to embark upon the Great Crusade." Later, just before the invasion was under way, he scrawled a note that he concealed from others and kept in his wallet, just in case. "Our landings . . . have failed," it began, and ended, "If any blame or fault attaches to the attempt it is mine alone."

On the evening of June 3 Stagg's prediction for the 5th was grim: unflyable weather, meaning no airborne drops. In effect, no invasion was possible on that day, since the one British and two American airborne divisions were essential to the operation's success. At the briefing on the evening of the fourth, Stagg held out a glimmer of hope; by the afternoon of the following day, he believed, skies would clear for about thirty-six hours. After feedback from the others, Ike pondered: to postpone again would mean no invasion until June 19, the first day tides would be right again. Then he made his decision: the 6th would be the day, subject to final approval the following morning. At 4 A.M. on June 5 the group met again in the now familiar mess room of Southwick House. Stagg remained optimistic, at least for the period of the initial invasion. Ike paced the floor getting opinions, but it was up to him. Finally, he turned to the group. "Okay, let's go." In less than a minute the room was cleared. Nothing could stop the invasion now. Its success was up to Ike's commanders and their forces, especially "the Boys of D-Day."

D-Day, June 6, 1944, a day for the history books. All Americans would remember where they were that day when they heard the news. Mamie was at West Point attending John's graduation. The Supreme Commander was in his headquarters keeping informed of developments in the assault area. The airborne divisions had accomplished their missions — disrupting enemy communications and movement until the ground forces could hook up with them — but their casualties were high. At Utah Beach, on the west flank of the invasion, the American forces achieved a measure of surprise, and casualties were relatively light. It was a different story for the American units on the adjacent Omaha Beach: they faced many bitter, bloody hours before they could establish the lodgement. Of the three British beaches to the east, Sword on the far flank was most threatening to the German forces and, hence, was the area in which they concentrated the bulk of their Normandy armor. The British Sixth Airborne Division secured that eastern flank at the cost in lives of almost half their attacking force.[6]

By nightfall the Allies had 133,000 men on what hours before, had been enemy territory. The cost was ten thousand casualties, about 25 percent of whom were dead. The Atlantic Wall had been breached. Despite the great achievement, this was no time for complacency. The holds on some beach areas, Omaha and Sword, were still precarious, and the weather, important to the continued flow of men and supplies through the beaches, remained unsettled. A week later, by which time the Allied position on the Continent was secure, the Soviet press published a handsome acknowledgment by Josef Stalin of the Allies' achievement. "One must admit that military history does not know a similar enterprise so broadly conceived on so huge a scale so masterfully executed."[7]

On June 7 Eisenhower crossed the channel to see things for himself and to meet with his senior commanders. Throughout the European campaigns Ike frequently visited the battle areas not only to talk to commanders at all levels but also with the soldiers themselves. In part the goal was to see and be seen by the troops, but it was more than that. The Supreme Commander felt it necessary to be intimately familiar with the tactical situation in order to make sound operational decisions when required. He particularly needed to see for himself when he received conflicting recommendations from his subordinate commanders. Some writers would later try to minimize Ike's role as a tactician, referring to him as a good organizer and coordinator, adept at the political level of decision making. He did indeed have those qualities, but he was also a superb tactician who made a point of having an intimate feel of the battle situation.

Within a few days of the landings American and British beachheads had linked up. Supplies and reinforcements continued to come in over the beaches, but a port was needed. The closest was Cherbourg at the end of the Cotentin peninsula. The task was assigned to the American VII Corps, which had tough going through the Norman hedgerows. It became a battle of attrition where progress was sometimes measured in yards. Finally, after fighting through strong points defending the port, they captured Cherbourg at the end of June, but the harbor had been demolished. It would not be operational until the end of August.

The slow Allied advance through hedgerow country fell far behind the SHAEF plan. Two major attacks were staged to help break out of the stabilized front. On July 8, after a heavy bombardment, Montgomery's forces attacked toward Caen, but they did not get far. Ten days later Montgomery attacked again, this time gaining about seven miles at the cost of six thousand casualties, but there was still no breakthrough. As it turned out, though, the Allies had an important gain: two panzer divisions due for commitment in the vicinity of Saint-Lô against American forces were diverted to hold the line in the British area.

In the American sector Bradley's forces had fought up to Saint-Lô. What they needed then was to break out and take advantage of the fourteen divisions Bradley had against the six the enemy had opposing him. There was also an increasing logistical imperative to expand out of the Normandy area, as the beachhead now contained some 1.5 million Allied soldiers and supplies were coming in at a favorable rate.[8]

To solve the breakout problem, Bradley came up with Operation Cobra, which began on July 25 with 2,500 aircraft bombing German positions. Some bombs fell short on American troops with disastrous results, but the bombardment wiped out the tough German division that stood in Bradley's way, the Panzer Lehr, and opened the way for American tanks, infantry, and artillery to pour through. On August 1 Ike activated the 12th Army Group, placing Bradley in charge and, on the same day, the Third U.S. Army with "Old Blood and Guts" Patton in charge. Thereafter, the advance was swift. Patton swept through Brittany, sent a column south to the Loire, and dispatched other columns east and north.

Not all of Ike's problems were at the front, though. Hardly was the breakout under way when Churchill, the strategist, was at it again. Anvil, the Allied landing in southern France, was scheduled for August 15. The goal was to sweep through southern France and link up with Ike's forces while at the same time providing the Allies the much-needed port of Marseilles. The prime minister pressed the Supreme Commander hard to cancel Anvil and to divert the forces to Italy. It was another one of his schemes to attack the "soft underbelly" of Europe, this time with the goal of reaching the Danube basin. Whatever Churchill's motives, the idea was a fantasy that would change the entire Overlord plan operationally and logistically. Standing up to the prime minister's cajoling, poetry, tears, and threats to resign, Eisenhower said no. As usual, when Churchill saw he could not get his way, he fully supported Anvil.

Hitler, having survived an attempt on his life on July 20, studied the situation in Normandy and—against the advice of his generals—ordered a counterattack to cut off Patton's breakout force. The U.S. First Army, along with Canadian, British, and Polish troops and supported by fighter bombers, defused it, then trapped the enemy forces in a pocket near Falaise. The Germans fought back hard. Although fifty thousand were captured and another ten thousand killed, many escaped eastward through the "Falaise gap."

The great race through France lasted for about a week, with the German forces retreating toward the Seine and the Allies in pursuit on either side of them. By August 19 Paris, anticipating the Allies' arrival, began an uprising. Its liberation on the 25th — with the French Second Armored Division leading the way into the City of Light — was the emotional peak of the war for the French nation. In southern France, meanwhile, Anvil was a success, with the U.S. Seventh Army pushing north for a September linkup with the Allied forces advancing from Normandy.

At this point, though, German resistance began to stiffen, and, since the Allies had temporarily outrun their supply capacity, Ike had to set priorities for his forces. The previous plan to advance on a broad front was now not feasible, at least until the supply situation improved. Montgomery wanted priority for his area in the north, while George Patton wanted it for the Third Army farther south. Ike compromised: Montgomery received priority, but Patton was allowed to go as far as available supplies could take his army. He was able to push forward about a hundred miles to the Meuse before the fuel supply ran out.

Farther north, British and Canadian forces advanced into the Netherlands, and American forces entered German territory after crossing Belgium and Luxembourg. But bad weather was coming, and unloading supplies over the Normandy beaches became much more difficult. Monty continued pushing for channeling all available resources into his area for a deep thrust into Germany. While Ike knew that this was a fantasy, he did approve one quick gamble — the seizure of a limited objective across the Rhine. This operation, called Market-Garden by Montgomery, involved dropping three airborne divisions. The U.S. 101st and 82nd would secure bridges for a dash of some sixty miles by a British armored force. That force would then link up with the British First Airborne Division dropped at Arnhem. The enemy reaction at Arnhem was fierce and the objective turned out to be

First-known photo of Dwight Eisenhower (1893). On the left is his oldest brother Arthur holding the baby Roy. Dwight stands in front of Edgar on the right. *Dwight D. Eisenhower Library*

Ike in action on the gridiron early in the 1912 season. At this point, he was one of West Point's outstanding football players. Later in the fall a knee injury during a game against Tufts cost him his football career. *Dwight D. Eisenhower Library*

A dignified and serious Ike in his formal cadet photograph in 1915.
He stood 125 out of 164 in his graduating class in demerits.
Dwight D. Eisenhower Library

Lieutenant Eisenhower married Mamie Geneva Doud at her parents'
house in Denver on July 1, 1916. Here the bride and groom pose for
their wedding picture. *Dwight D. Eisenhower Library*

Eisenhower's inability to see any combat during World War I was a
source of frustration for him. Instead he trained men in the primitive
tanks of the day. Captain Eisenhower is pictured here with one of
these early machines at Camp Meade, Maryland, in 1919.
US Army photo courtesy of the Dwight D. Eisenhower Library

Major Eisenhower in 1933 at the new Army Industrial College, which he helped establish while an assistant to Chief of Staff Douglas MacArthur. *US Army*

Douglas MacArthur, military adviser to the Philippines, (center) is
flanked by his aides T. J. Davis (left) and Dwight Eisenhower during
a ceremony at Malacanang Palace in 1935.
Dwight D. Eisenhower Library

Eisenhower, now chief of staff, Third Army, Fort Sam Houston, Texas, standing with his boss Lt. Gen. Walter Krueger (left) as they arrive at Lake Charles, Louisiana, to begin the 1941 maneuvers. The perspiring officer on the right is Lt. Col. Oliver H. Stout, commanding officer of the 113th Observation Squadron.

US Army photo courtesy of the Dwight D. Eisenhower Library

Eisenhower in London in late September 1942 with his chief of staff, Brig. Gen. Walter Bedell Smith (standing, left), who remained with him the entire war, and Maj. Gen. Mark Clark, Ike's deputy.
US Army photo courtesy of the Dwight D. Eisenhower Library

Two days after his appointment to command the cross-channel invasion, Eisenhower conferred with the president aboard the presidential airplane *The Sacred Cow* en route to Sicily (December 8, 1943). *Dwight D. Eisenhower Library*

In this famous photograph, Eisenhower visits with the men of
Company E, 502d Parachute Infantry Regiment, 101st Airborne
Division late in the day on June 5, 1944. The airborne units would
be the first Allied troops into Normandy on D-Day. *US Army*

Eisenhower meeting with Bernard Montgomery (left), then commander of the 21st Army Group, and Omar Bradley who headed the
12th Army Group (fall 1944). The two commanders could not have
been more different in personality: Montgomery was flamboyant and
temperamental, while Bradley was quiet and calm to the point of
stoicism. *US Army photo courtesy of the Dwight D. Eisenhower Library*

Eisenhower and three of his field commanders (l to r Patton, Bradley, and Courtney Hodges) meet as the war nears its final stages. Patton was justifiably elated: his mighty Third Army was moving into the history books as one of the greatest western armies of all time.
US Army photo courtesy of the Dwight D. Eisenhower Library

Eisenhower throwing out the ceremonial first pitch to open the 1957
season at a game between the Washington Senators and the Baltimore
Orioles. Behind him on the right is Vice President Richard Nixon.
National Park Service photo courtesy of the Dwight D. Eisenhower Library

Cold War diplomacy. The Khrushchevs visited the United States and were feted at a state dinner at the White House on September 15, 1959. *US Navy photo courtesy of the Dwight D. Eisenhower Library*

Eisenhower conferring with LBJ on board Air Force One in February 1968.
Dwight D. Eisenhower Library

a "bridge too far" for the Allies. Aside from the operation's failure to achieve its objective, it had also diverted resources that could have been used for opening the port of Antwerp, logistically vital to any sustained Allied combat in Germany.

The campaign in France, even though it ended on the Arnhem misadventure, is one of the great campaigns in Western military history. Under Eisenhower's direction France and Belgium were liberated and the German forces severely weakened. This weakening of the enemy was true elsewhere: in Italy the Nazis were barely holding on in the Apennines, and in the east the Soviets were at the frontiers of the Third Reich. Still the German Army remained a dangerous foe, both in capability and fighting spirit.

In his role as Supreme Commander, Eisenhower was by now a world figure, conveying to the public and press the image of an amiable, upbeat chairman-of-the-board personality. In his role as commander of American forces, however, he reflected another aspect of his personality: a confident, aggressive, strong leader, but quick to give public praise to those subordinates who merited it. In practice he had less authority over Allied subordinates than over American, but this was not a problem except in the case of Monty, recently promoted to field marshal. Churchill had done this to assuage the general's feelings when Ike assumed personal control of the ground forces on September 1. The Monty problem came to a head that fall over his failure to open access to the vital port of Antwerp. Ike, who should have forced the issue earlier, finally lost patience. He put the stick to Montgomery, who was still reluctant to commit the necessary forces, and insisted the port be opened. Backing down, the field marshal finally deployed enough strength to clear German troops from the approach area and thus open the port to receive supplies.[9]

As Ike moved his three Army groups (Monty's 21st, Bradley's 12th, and Dever's Sixth) forward, the action became a battle of attrition all along the broad front. The Allies also faced the worst European weather in thirty years. Many weeks of bloody fighting in mud, snow, and increasing cold took its toll on troop strength and morale. Along the line of contact, though, the Ardennes Forest was judged to be a relatively quiet area; there some of the battle-weary units could recover, and units new to Europe gain some seasoning. The view at SHAEF was that in terrain like the Ardennes, no heavy fighting would occur during the approaching winter.

On the morning of December 16 Ike arrived at his office in SHAEF — now located in a hotel in Versailles — to find a message from Washington announcing his promotion to the newly established five-star rank of General of the Army. Two others receiving this rank were George Marshall and Ike's old boss, Douglas MacArthur. Also on the schedule that day was a happy event: the marriage of Sgt. "Mickey" McKeough, who had been with Ike since 1941, to WAC Cpl. Pearlie Hargreaves, a member of the office staff. Afterward, the Supreme Commander returned to his map-cluttered office for a meeting with Bradley to discuss the shortage of combat troop replacements. As the meeting got under way, an interruption came from the SHAEF intelligence chief, British Maj. Gen. Ken Strong, with reports coming in of a major German attack in the Ardennes.

Hitler was making this last desperate attempt to reverse the situation on the western front. During the fall battles the Germans had been secretly concentrating their forces to create two new panzer armies for this assault. Their goal was to cut across the Ardennes to the Meuse River and then drive to the northwest to seize Antwerp, thereby cutting off Montgomery's Army Group from Bradley's. Von Rundstedt, the German commander, had been waiting for a period of bad weather that would keep the Allied Air Forces grounded—a necessity to achieve a successful assault. That came on December 16.

German success at the outset was striking, shattering two American divisions and moving forward about thirty-five miles in the first few days. By the 18th, the magnitude of the attack was clear to Eisenhower, and he took a number of decisive steps. On the northern side of the German penetration, or bulge, he placed Monty in temporary command of Bradley's First and Ninth

Armies, since Bradley's headquarters was too far away. In the south he ordered Patton to have the Third Army do an abrupt ninety-degree turn and attack into the bulge. This would relieve the surrounded 101st Airborne, placed in the town of Bastogne to prevent the Germans from securing a major crossroads. On the 22nd Ike issued one of his few Orders of the Day: Repulsing the enemy would not be enough—"destroy him!"[10]

By Christmas Day the German advance had been halted. They were still five miles short of the Meuse after having penetrated sixty miles. The following day, Allied forces attacked from the northern side of the bulge; in the south Patton's Third Army reached the surrounded 101st at Bastogne. Worst of all for the Germans, the skies cleared, allowing the Allied Air Forces to strike at will.

The dark December was over. Hitler's attempt to reenact his great breakthrough in the Ardennes in 1940 had failed. By the middle of January the Germans had been pushed back to where they had started. The Battle of the Bulge, as it had become known, was over. Losses were heavy on both sides, 100,000 Germans and 81,000 Allies—of which 71,000 were American—but there was a difference. The Allies could make up the losses, while Hitler could not. To add to the Nazis' plight, on January 12 the Soviets opened an offensive that would carry them to within forty miles of Berlin. Whatever forces Hitler could salvage from his Ardennes offensive, he now had to shift eastward.

Eisenhower's decisive response to the crisis had been far swifter than the Germans had anticipated. His intuitive judgment on how to counter the assault had turned out to be correct; he had, in effect, taken control of the battle. As if the problem of contending with two panzer armies was not enough, he also had to contend with two senior subordinates playing the role of prima donnas. In a scene Gilbert and Sullivan would have envied, Bradley threatened to resign when told that Montgomery was assuming temporary control of two of his armies. Ike settled that one easily: "Brad . . . your resignation means nothing."[11] (In effect, get back to work.) The problems with Monty were more

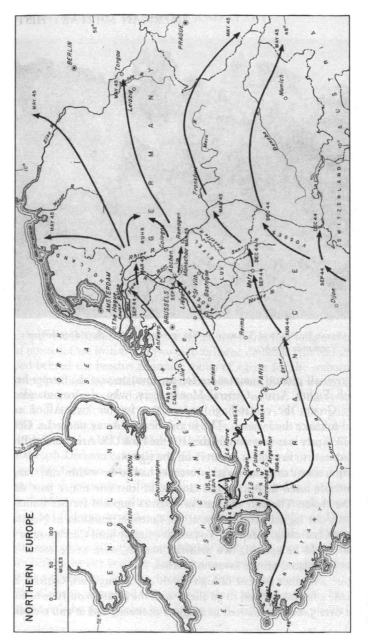

Allied Operations in Northern Europe, 1944–1945.

time consuming: Ike had to prod him to speed up his counter-attack against the German penetration. He also had to defuse Montgomery's attempt to have Ike change his overall strategy from a broad front attack to a single thrust into Germany (which, of course, would have been under Monty's command). The field marshal did, however, manage to get in a press conference explaining how he won the Battle of the Bulge and allowing that American GIs made great fighting men when given proper — meaning Monty's — leadership. American officers who heard of this comment, including Bradley and Patton, were outraged.

On February 7 the Allies began their campaign to eliminate enemy forces west of the Rhine. Though the Germans continued to fight hard and at times with fanaticism, there was no way that they could now withstand the weight of the Allied assault. What was left of their strength slowly eroded, and within a month Eisenhower's forces were on the Rhine from Nijmegen in the north all the way to Coblenz. Then came one of the great breaks in the war: The American Ninth Armored Division seized the last intact bridge over the Rhine at Remagen; before the Ludendorff Bridge collapsed, Ike poured five divisions over it.

Farther south the Third and Seventh Armies launched coordi-nated attacks to capture the remaining part of the Rhineland, and on March 21 Patton was over the great river at Oppenheim. Beginning on the 23rd Montgomery launched his long-planned Operation Plunder, involving crossings of the river by British and American forces. They were supported by the war's largest air-borne landings, but that was probably mainly for show; by the time the troops descended, the landing zones were already in the hands of British troops.

During Plunder, Eisenhower was at Montgomery's headquar-ters for a quick visit, as was Churchill. In the course of discus-sions with Ike the prime minister opined that the Allies should try to beat the Russians to Berlin. Ike thought not; thus was raised what was perhaps the last great controversy of World War II for the Supreme Commander. Both Eisenhower and Churchill had good reasons for their positions. Churchill's were primarily political, while Ike's were from the point of view of a Supreme Commander concerned about unnecessary casualties to his forces. Holding to his position despite subsequent badgering by Churchill, Ike was backed by Marshall. In future years, though, the issue was to plague Eisenhower.

By April the long trail that had begun years before was nearing its end — an end that Commander in Chief Roosevelt did not live to see. He died on April 12. At times the Germans fought hard as the Allies poured over their country, but they had only about twenty-five divisions to combat almost eighty Allied. The Canadians cleared Holland, and the British drove for Hamburg and the lower Elbe. The American First and Ninth Armies also headed for the Elbe. Patton's Third moved toward Czechoslovakia, then south down the Danube Valley and into Austria, while the American Seventh and French First also moved into southern Germany and then into Austria. Throughout the month the horror of the Nazi concentration camps was exposed as camp after camp was overrun by the Allies. By April 27 the Russians had completely encircled Berlin, and three days later Hitler committed suicide.

On May 7, 1945, eleven months and one day after the landings in Normandy, the war ended in Eisenhower's headquarters, a schoolhouse in Reims, France. Field Marshal Alfred Jodl signed the instrument of surrender for the defeated Nazis. After tiring of his staff officers' efforts to write a grandiloquent message to the combined American and British Chiefs of Staff, officially informing them of the surrender, Ike quickly wrote one in his own hand: "The mission of this allied force was fulfilled at 0241 local time, May 7, 1945." The Great Crusade was over.

Chapter 5

Road to the White House

T HE WAR IN Europe, which had been going on for almost six years, was finally over, and the Allies set about feting the victorious generals. On June 10 Soviet Marshal Zhukov presented Ike the Soviets' highest award — the Order of Victory. The most impressive ceremony was in London two days later. Millions cheered as he rode in an open carriage to the historic Guildhall, where he made the principal speech to an audience that included most high-ranking military and civilian officials in the United Kingdom. Then on June 14 a million Parisians cheered him during a ceremony at the Arc de Triomphe.

On June 18 he arrived at Washington National Airport to the shouts of "Ike, Ike." Mamie met the plane, but there was time only for a brief kiss and hug before he was whisked away to address a joint session of Congress. The following morning in New York four million people greeted him as he rode through the streets of Manhattan. Then a few days later he was back in Abilene, where it had all started. A frail Ida was there along with his brothers. At this point Ike was not only a national hero, but an international figure as well. No wonder so many Americans were already thinking of him as a potential president.

After the celebrations at home Ike returned to Frankfurt to the anticlimactic role of heading the American occupation zone and forces. Shortly after the German surrender, Ike had written to Mamie that he was hoping she could join him in Europe during the occupation. Eisenhower later tried that out with Marshall, who in return took the request to President Truman, who said no, not until the wives of others could join their husbands in Europe.

On July 15 Ike welcomed Truman to Europe. The president was on his way to Potsdam to meet with Churchill and Stalin. Though Eisenhower had no significant role in that final summit meeting of the war, he did meet with the President on several occasions. During one such meeting Truman indicated that he would support Ike for the presidency in 1948 should he decide to run. Ike later wrote that he treated the President's offer as a very splendid joke. Perhaps on both sides the communication could be viewed as an early move in what was going to be a long chess game.

With the dropping of the two atomic bombs on Japan in August, followed by that country's surrender, the war was really over. The American troops in Europe wanted to go home, and deployments proceeded as fast as ships became available. The remaining American occupation forces headed by Ike faced a huge problem: how to provide relief for the German population and the millions of displaced persons who roamed about the ravaged German landscape trying to find something to eat and a way to get home, if they still had one. Almost all food supplies had to be brought in from the outside, and disease swept the desolate country. These problems would take a long time to solve, but on November 19, 1945, Ike was summoned home to replace George Marshall as Army Chief of Staff.

Normally, this position would be the pinnacle of an Army officer's career. Not in Ike's case. There had never been a job like that of Supreme Commander; no other military duty could match the demands of Operation Overlord. Furthermore, while Eisenhower did find challenges as Army chief, they were frequently not the type of problem that was truly solvable or that gave much satisfaction in trying.

The main task facing him was demobilization. Neither the service personnel nor their families believed that the United States needed to maintain a major military force. The war was over, and its veterans wanted to return to their civilian pursuits. Eisenhower received a flood of mail, especially from parents who wanted their "boys" home. By the end of June 1947, when the demobilization officially ended, the American military force of twelve million had fallen to 1.5 million. As President Truman said, this was disintegration, not demobilization.

Reconverting the Army to a peacetime economy was a further problem. Amid inflation and tight budgets, Chief of Staff Eisenhower had to fight for the Army's slice of a very small pie. Another battle raged over the future organization of the armed forces. This was finally settled by the National Security Act of 1947, a Navy legislative victory. The act called for a loose, federalized arrangement of the three services — Army, Navy, Air Force — under a secretary of defense with limited authority. As if all this were not enough, the Cold War began during Ike's years as Chief of Staff. One of its significant by-products was the Truman Doctrine of March 1947, leading to the American policy of containment to check the "expansion" of communism.

Tremendously busy with all these concerns, Ike traveled widely and, whenever possible, with Mamie. In the fall of 1947 a United Press reporter tracked him down at a castle in Ayrshire, Scotland, soon after the sentences of the Nazi leadership were announced at the conclusion of the Nuremberg trials. On the whole Ike seemed pleased with the verdicts, although surprised at the ease with which the military leadership was convicted. The reporter asked: "If the war had gone the other way, General, do you think that they would have hanged you?" "Such thoughts you have, young man," Ike replied.[1]

For every speech he made, he had to turn down forty others. Most Americans saw him as a possible candidate for president, but he still denied any interest. Pleasant events were happening, too. In June 1947 John Eisenhower married Barbara Thompson, herself an "Army brat." The following March, Ike and Mamie became grandparents with the birth of a namesake, Dwight David Eisenhower II.

By the spring of 1947 Ike was becoming eager to leave active duty. But what would he do? It was too early for serious presidential campaigning, especially with Truman still in the running. Ike had several discussions with Thomas J. Watson, president of IBM, and a member of the search committee to select a successor to Nicholas Murray Butler, who had presided for fifty years as president of Columbia University in New York. Watson was interested in getting Ike to seek the Republican nomination for president in the future, but for the interim, how about the presidency of Columbia? Finally, Ike, who had had enough of being Chief of Staff, relented and accepted with certain conditions, including no responsibility for fund-raising.

Meanwhile, publishers were pressuring Ike for his memoirs of the war. Thus, in early February 1948 he turned over his duties as Chief of Staff to his successor, Gen. Omar Bradley, and returned on terminal leave to the seclusion of Fort Myer's Quarters One. There, with the help of supporting staff, he wrote his first book in only three months. *Crusade in Europe* was well received and, thanks to Truman, the money received from the publisher was treated as a capital gain, taxed at one-third the rate of ordinary income. The difference made Ike a wealthy man.

On the first Sunday in May 1948 the Eisenhowers left Fort Myer and the Army for their first civilian home, settling in the house provided for the president of Columbia adjoining the New York City campus. Ike's formal induction took place at a convocation on October 12, 1948. Ike was now in a strange new world of trustees, deans, academics, and students. All in all, although as an outsider he was the butt of many of the professors' jokes, Ike handled himself adequately in this unfamiliar environment. And in his thirty-two months at Columbia, he managed to juggle his duties at the university with an extraordinary amount of private political activity. As befit a potential presidential candidate, he met frequently with Republican influentials.

When President Truman unexpectedly defeated Republican candidate Thomas Dewey in 1948, there was no question as to who was the long-range winner: Dwight Eisenhower. Had Dewey been elected, he might have been president for the next eight years. By then Ike would have been sixty-six and probably out of the limelight. The Democratic victory therefore opened the doors to Ike as a Republican candidate in 1952.

Flaring up during Ike's Columbia years was a major international event, the Korean War. Shortly after North Korean communists invaded South Korea on June 25, 1950, Truman committed U.S. forces. By September, after early losses, they had broken through with MacArthur's end run at Inchon but were pushed back inside South Korea again when the Chinese intervened in November. The war, though a limited one, was to drag on for three years. Reserves were called up, and the economy suffered. In time the war became unpopular and so did Truman, who seemed unable to bring it to an end. That would play an important part in the 1952 election.

Of more immediate significance to Ike, however, were events in Europe set in motion by the Korean War. At first perceived as part of a worldwide communist offensive, the Korean War galvanized the North Atlantic Treaty Organization. NATO had been organized in April 1949 after a succession of Soviet actions, especially the Czechoslovakian coup of February 1948 and the Berlin blockade of 1948–49. With Korea, NATO members saw the need to establish a military infrastructure to guard against a Soviet attack in Europe. When NATO set up the military position of Supreme Allied Commander (SACEUR), what better person could fill it than Eisenhower, the old wartime hero? It was not a bad place for a potential presidential candidate to be, either. Taking a leave of absence from Columbia, Ike assumed his new command at Supreme Headquarters near Paris on January 7, 1951.

Eisenhower's SACEUR duties were more political than those of his wartime command. Among other things he needed to lend his prestige in order to build support for a common defense among the twelve NATO nations. This meant dealing with old national animosities, as well as convincing the people of the NATO countries to believe in the cause enough to meet their share of the defense requirements.

Ike also used this time to refine and expand on the political contacts he had made during the Columbia years and to develop his own public position on international and domestic issues. Because of his experience, his international views came naturally; here he had a clear-cut edge over his chief potential rival in the Republican Party, Sen. Robert Taft. Ike's views on domestic matters were less developed, except for one certain and often-stated position: the strength and integrity of the American economy and financial structure must be preserved.

During the seventeen months Ike was a chief player on the NATO stage, he received a great deal of political prodding to become an announced Republican candidate. Finally, in January 1952 he acknowledged that he was a Republican, and in March let Sen. Henry Cabot Lodge enter his name in the New Hampshire presidential primary. This ended the cordial relationship he had maintained with Truman over the years.

On June 1, 1952, Ike left NATO and the miliary service to become an active candidate. He began his campaign for the presidency with an undistinguished speech in Abilene but made up for it with an outstanding press conference the next day. Eisenhower still had tough going against Taft, but at the July convention in Chicago, with its ubiquitous "I like Ike" signs, Republicans made him their standard-bearer. The selection of Richard Milhous Nixon of California as his running mate soon posed a dilemma for Ike with the disclosure that Nixon might have improperly accepted campaign money from businessmen. The vice presidential candidate overcame that problem with his famous Checkers speech of September 23, 1952.

Other difficulties arose during Ike's whistle-stop campaign (he was the last president to campaign extensively by train), especially when Sen. Joseph McCarthy made some snide and false charges against Ike's old mentor George Marshall, portraying him as a Soviet agent. Eisenhower's failure to defend Marshall at this point was probably the nadir of his campaign; however, the three buzzwords with which the Republican candidate charged the Democrats — Korea, communism, and corruption — were highly effective. On October 24 in Detroit, Ike announced that after the election he would go to Korea, presumably to bring an end to the war. That was what the Americans wanted to hear, and from then on Ike was "in."

On election day, November 4, 1952, Dwight Eisenhower received 55 percent of the popular vote. The electoral vote was 442 for him, 89 for his Democratic opponent, Adlai Stevenson. When Stevenson conceded in the early morning hours, one of Ike's first actions was to call former President Herbert Hoover, who had left the White House twenty years before, during the Great Depression, and was the last Republican to have held the job.

Less than a month after the election he set out on his promised trip to Korea. The visit reinforced Eisenhower's determination to terminate the war one way or another. In his words, "One possibility was to let the Communist authorities understand that, in the absence of satisfactory progress, we intended to move decisively without inhibition in our use of weapons, and would no longer be responsible for confining hostilities to the Korean peninsula. We would not be limited by any worldwide gentleman's agreement."[2]

Chapter 6

Mr. President

J ANUARY 20, 1953. From the north portico of the White House and up Pennsylvania Avenue rode outgoing President Harry S Truman and the man who was replacing him, Dwight David Eisenhower, the first Republican president in twenty years. The ride to the Capitol was frosty, as much from Ike's reaction to Truman's earlier characterization of his Korean trip — Truman called it demagoguery — as from the chilly weather.

After being sworn in by Chief Justice Fred Vinson, Ike gave Mamie a kiss. Returning to the rostrum and wearing his big grin, he threw his arms in the air in the V sign. The new President — buoyant, cheerful, sunny, and seemingly uncomplicated — was the ultimate folk hero of his time. Devoting his short inaugural address mainly to foreign policy matters, he made only passing reference to domestic issues. The next day many newspapers noted that the speech repudiated isolationism and signaled the right wing of his party that the new administration must relate more to a changing world.

In one area, though, the new President's views agreed with most of his party — his conservative economic views. These views were genuine and of long standing. John Eisenhower says that they originated during his father's first Washington tour in the late 1920s when he worked on industrial mobilization. They were nurtured during the Columbia years by a number of Republicans who were pushing him for the presidency. It should be noted, nonetheless, that many far-right Republicans thought him too liberal. While Ike may have had misgivings about the principle of the welfare state, he made no attempt to turn the clock back. In his first State of the Union message on February 2 the new President asked for an expansion of social security; before long he was asking for a "soil bank" for farmers and federal aid for education. Ike was a conservative but he was not a reactionary.

As Ike later set forth in his memoirs, he brought to the presidency certain strategic concepts: to rely on deterrence and rule out preventive war; to stress the role of nuclear technology and to reduce reliance on U.S. conventional forces; to place heavy emphasis on Allied land forces around the Soviet periphery; to stress economic strength, especially through reduced defense budgets; and to be prepared to continue the struggle with the USSR over decades.

Given these strategic views and the domestic and international constraints Ike perceived, how could he blend them into a credible strategy that could be implemented at a relatively low cost? There was also the question of selling it to both the American public and America's allies. To help accomplish this, Ike chose his key appointees with great care. Three were of particular importance. His selection of John Foster Dulles as secretary of state was not inevitable, but neither was it surprising. Dulles had campaigned long and hard for the office, and his talents for such a position were not inconsiderable. He had spent most of his life as a highly successful Wall Street lawyer specializing in international cases. In 1944 he became presidential candidate Thomas Dewey's chief adviser on foreign policy. This role inaugurated his association with government that continued for the rest of his life.

Another Ike appointee — and the only one except for Dulles with whom he established a close relationship — was the secretary of the treasury, George Magoffin Humphrey. He arrived in Washington with a "passion for the domestic economy" in keeping with his conservative business background. Of great value to him in Cabinet meetings were his debating skill, aggressive manner, and strong convictions.

Charles E. Wilson, Eisenhower's choice for secretary of defense, was the highly successful president of General Motors who, in his own field, exhibited a powerful and confident personality. Bluff and colorful in manner, he was prone to making highly quotable statements of a type not designed to enhance his relations with Congress. When he arrived at the Pentagon, his insight into foreign affairs and strategic issues was negligible, and he did not seem to gain much sophistication in the office. As time went on, "Engine Charlie" declined in influence with the President, while the other two powerful men in the Cabinet, Dulles and Humphrey, greatly increased their influence. In filling his remaining Cabinet posts, Eisenhower tended toward wealthy businessmen. One exception was Martin Durkin, who had been head of the plumbers' union, hence the quip that the Cabinet consisted of "nine millionaires and a plumber."

Eisenhower's immense popularity had been a central factor in his election, but equally important were two of his campaign pledges: to end the Korean War and to reduce the role of the federal government in American life. This latter point was perhaps more effective as rhetoric than as a guide to economic policy, but its real intent was reduced and balanced budgets.

On taking office Ike, a newcomer to politics and his party, was dependent on Republican leadership in the Eighty-third Congress, especially that of Senator Taft, Mr. Republican. Anticipating this, Ike had visited his defeated rival immediately after his nomination and had said of him, "His willingness to cooperate is absolutely necessary to the success of the Republican Party in the campaign and in the administration to follow."[1] The two began formal negotiations for cooperation at a breakfast meeting in September. Taft brought along a proposed statement of understanding that included a budgetary goal of $70 billion, down from Truman's $75 billion.

In the spring, when Eisenhower presented his actual budget to the cabinet, it was higher than Taft's goal. The senator, who was present, was outraged. "We'll never elect a Republican Congress in 1954," he thundered. Taft eventually came around to supporting Ike's proposal; not long after, however, the senator was diagnosed with terminal cancer. He died at the end of July.

With Taft's unexpected departure Ike found his relationship with Congress much more difficult, and increasingly he had to seek Democratic backing for his programs. To bring the legislators around to his point of view, Eisenhower depended on his considerable abilities of persuasion and compromise. That proved to be good practice for what was to come: the Eighty-third Congress was the only one of the four during Ike's presidency that was Republican-controlled.

On March 4, 1953, six weeks after his inauguration, Ike learned that Stalin was seriously ill; by the next day he was dead. This was end-of-an-era stuff, but what to do? After some going back and forth with his advisers Ike approved a pro forma statement. It set forth what amounted to a prayer for "peace and comradeship" but included no specific peace overtures.

About ten days later Malenkov, Stalin's successor for the moment, issued a conciliatory statement that required a reply in some way from the President. How about a speech by Ike? Thus was born what has been called perhaps the finest speech of his presidency, titled "The Chance for Peace." It was also a superior bit of Cold War propaganda.

On April 16 Ike delivered the speech to the American Society of Newspaper Editors in Washington. Suffering from what turned out to be an attack of ileitis, Ike gripped the lectern and gave a bravura performance. "Every gun that is made, every warship launched, every rocket fired signifies, in the final sense, a theft from those who hunger and are not fed, those who are cold and are not clothed."

Here was a former general of the Army stating that "the cost of one heavy bomber is a modern brick school in more than thirty cities" or "two fine, fully equipped hospitals." He then aimed some proposals directly at the Kremlin that would, if carried out, presumably turn bombers into schools and hospitals. In effect, he was asking if the Soviets were ready to negotiate agreements for controlling atomic energy and prohibiting atomic weapons. Coming when they did, the proposals were startling. For the moment, though, no real Soviet leadership was in place to respond, even had the Kremlin wished. Still, the reception to the speech in the Western world was overwhelmingly favorable.

As events outside the United States, especially the death of Stalin, were changing the diplomatic environment, the administration considered various options in Korea. Ike, of course, knew what he wanted, if he could achieve it: to redeem his pledge to end the war that had become highly unpopular with the American public and had already cost America almost 28,000 battle deaths.

In Panmunjom both sides were negotiating seriously on the complex problem of those Chinese and North Korean prisoners who did not want to return home. By June 8, with an agreement hammered out establishing a Neutral Nations Repatriation Commission, which eventually released those who did not wish to return home, all that was left to the negotiators was to establish a cease-fire line. One influential person, though, did not agree — Syngman Rhee, the seventy-seven-year-old leader of South Korea who wanted to continue the fighting. On June 19 he released some 25,000 prisoners (about half of whom had no desire to go home), a direct violation of the tentative agreement with the Chinese.

At a cabinet meeting with the President, Secretary of State Dulles thought that Rhee had a legitimate point, echoing some Republican influentials who thought that the United States should go for a battlefield victory in the war. Ike would have none of that and insisted on negotiating with Rhee. Finally, some promises were made to Rhee, such as a mutual security pact with South Korea and millions of dollars in food and economic aid.

On July 9 came additional pressure on Rhee from the Chinese: the People's Liberation Army began a strong offensive into the South Korean sector of the front. When the offensive sent a couple of South Korean divisions reeling, Rhee got the message.

On July 11 he publicly announced his support for the truce, and by the 27th all the details had been worked out. That night for the first time in more than three years the guns went silent and the killing ended on the Korean front. Many years after he left the White House Ike listed the ending of the war as one of his greatest achievements. He was right.

With the war in Korea over, Ike decided that it was time to bring American strategic policy and the supporting defense budget in line with his own views. On October 13, 1953, Defense Secretary Wilson presented the proposed defense budget for fiscal year 1955 to the President at a meeting of the National Security Council (NSC). Wilson was proposing a defense budget of $42 billion, no substantial change from the previous year. The reaction of Treasury Secretary Humphrey, who along with Ike expected a defense budget of about $36 billion, was what one source called "horrified."[2]

It fell to the new Joint Chiefs of Staff Chairman Adm. Arthur Radford to defend the military position. Instead, he centered his discussion on the need for additional presidential guidance on the employment of nuclear weapons if the defense budget was to be reduced. His message, which really reflected his own and the Air Force's views, not the views of the other services, was to have very significant results. If using nuclear weapons from the outset of a conflict was accepted as a planning premise, he said, then a less costly defense force could indeed be developed.

This approach, which in fact also reflected Ike's views, led to a subsequent NSC session with the President in late October at which Eisenhower approved a landmark document: NSC 162/2, the policy statement of what became known as Ike's "New Look" strategy. The policy, based on Radford's suggestion at the earlier meeting, placed maximum reliance on nuclear weapons to deter war; however, if that failed to deter, then nuclear weapons could be used. By late 1953 Eisenhower had established a strategic policy to fit his budgetary goals, and the New Look, with some later modification, would remain the basic defense policy during his presidency, though not without some strong challenges.

The first challenge came from outside the government. Books

and articles, mainly the work of academics, at first emphasized the lack of limited-war capabilities; later, these criticisms centered on the need to provide the capability for a gradual escalation before employing nuclear weapons. In aggregate, the authors' argument was for a wider spectrum of options before resorting to massive retaliation (Dulles's term used in a January 1954 speech). Eisenhower probably paid no attention to the criticisms, but they did provide support for the opponents to his strategy.

A second challenge came from the bureaucracy, in particular the Army and Navy. The Air Force was relatively content, since under the New Look it received 46 percent of the defense budget. Though the arguments were couched in doctrinal terms, they were really about budgetary resources. In dealing with the senior military on this issue, Ike used one of his successful leadership techniques — avoidance of public confrontation. Specifically, he insisted that defense issues not be subject to public debate. His military appointees had first to undergo a kind of loyalty test to convince him of their willingness to support his policies. Another technique Ike employed was to try to convert the doubters at NSC and at other meetings by constantly preaching that a sound economy — meaning low defense budgets — was the real basis of national security.

The third and most important challenge came from both houses of Congress, where the military had its allies. Using various techniques to protect his strategic program, Ike did well in gaining and keeping legislative support for his policies. Besides his personal persuasion of individual members of Congress, he established guidelines for the bureaucracy in their congressional testimony. In later times this might have been interpreted as stretching executive privilege or perhaps muzzling. He wanted no testimony on matters under consideration and no testimony on how specific decisions were made. In the main, Eisenhower's basic power in dealing with Congress lay in his wide public support. In matters of defense, the American public perceived him to be the most important military figure of his time.

Though Ike had opted for a nuclear-heavy strategy, he viewed the New Look primarily as a deterrent to war rather than a war-fighting strategy — a fine point, to be sure, from the perspective of a potential adversary. During that same fall of 1953 the public learned that the Soviets had recently tested a hydrogen bomb. To allay public fear, Eisenhower decided on an address to the United Nations proposing that the United States and the USSR work together toward peaceful uses of nuclear power. This speech, "Atoms for Peace," to the General Assembly on December 8, 1953, also included a proposal to diminish the world's atomic stockpiles.

In the United Nations and elsewhere, Ike's speech was greeted enthusiastically, but not much came from it. The Soviets stalled; after all, even with reducing atomic weapons the United States still had a big lead. The American follow-through was not very convincing either: in March 1954, only three months after Ike's talk, a U.S. test explosion in the South Pacific resulted in a pall of radioactive material over the Marshall Islands. In the end, Ike's "Atoms for Peace" never became a reality.

Another problem very much on the President's mind in the winter of 1953–54 was Indochina. His administration had inherited Truman's policy of support for the French in their attempts to suppress a Vietnamese revolution led by Ho Chi Minh. Ike had also accepted the Truman concept that Ho's organization was an instrument of international communism and that the fall of French Indochina would trigger the loss of all Southeast Asia with disastrous strategic consequences for the West — the "Domino Theory."

In early 1954 Ho's forces, led by General Vo Nguyen Giap, surrounded a French garrison at Dien Bien Phu. Given the unpopularity of the war in France at this point, observers of the French political scene felt that the loss of this garrison might lead to a withdrawal of the French from Indochina. The problem, as Ike saw it, was not the fate of Dien Bien Phu per se, but rather how to keep the French in the fight even if Dien Bien Phu were to fall. Direct American intervention, which the French requested, would, however, be another matter. With the Korean War still a fresh sore spot in the minds of the American public, Ike would need endorsement from Capitol Hill for such an action; however, Congress made clear that it would not be forthcoming unless other allies, meaning Britain, became involved. Busy dismantling their own empire, the British could hardly be expected to assist the French in keeping theirs. Ike said no to France.

On May 7 came the final transmission from the surrounded French garrison: "Fini, fini, fini." France's will to continue the war collapsed. On July 20 in Geneva a truce was signed that ended hostilities and fixed a demarcation line at the 17th parallel. Below it was established what came to be known as South Vietnam. In the immediate post-Geneva period, South Vietnam became a jungle of political factions, both religious and secular. Into this mishmash the Eisenhower administration expanded American support with the goal of stabilizing South Vietnam and also Southeast Asia.

Early in 1955 the President approved military assistance in terms of matériel and advisers to the new South Vietnamese government. This was a benchmark in America's involvement; in effect, the United States was officially propping up an independent South Vietnam. During the middle and late 1950s the United States reorganized, equipped, and trained the South Vietnamese army, besides supplying millions in foreign aid. The effect on the new state was forced dependency rather than genuine independence, which in any case it probably could not have handled. In sum, while Ike kept America out of war in Indochina, he continued and then accelerated Truman's policies, thus getting the United States more deeply involved in Vietnam.

Not all of Ike's problems were international. There were the everyday pressures of domestic issues, such as farm prices, aid to education, housing, and more. Then there was the matter of McCarthyism, the term given to the tactics of the junior senator from Wisconsin, Joseph McCarthy. Since the 1952 election McCarthy, a World War II Marine veteran, had chaired a Senate committee investigating government operations. Starting back in 1950, when he publicly announced that he had a list of communists in the State Department, McCarthy had been busy destroying reputations, careers, families, and sometimes lives with his reckless — and in most cases fictional — charges. His casualties were not just government officials, but also college professors, newspaper and television reporters, and people in the movie industry. Operating under the cloak of congressional immunity, in time he threatened the integrity of America's political and judicial systems.

Ike felt that the best way to suppress McCarthy was to refuse to confront his fellow Republican directly, to ignore him. He did, though, take swipes at McCarthy during press conferences and on other occasions. Eisenhower believed that the Senate itself should handle the McCarthy problem, and it did so eventually, but not before the senator had ruined many livelihoods. While Eisenhower's handling of the McCarthy affair was not his greatest moment, in the end, McCarthy did as Ike had predicted; he destroyed himself.

In the months before the 1954 midterm elections Ike campaigned vigorously. Aiming to continue his party's control of Congress, he managed some forty speeches and ten thousand miles of political trips. Despite his efforts and those of Vice President Richard Nixon, the Republicans lost seventeen seats in the House and two in the Senate, enough to give Democrats control of both houses. For a midterm election the results were not surprising; in fact, Ike's efforts had probably prevented an even greater loss. As the *New York Times* put it:

> The President's personal standing with the voters seemed largely intact. Although his exceptionally vigorous campaigning did not save Congress for the Republicans, it was credited with averting a heavier Democratic sweep.[3]

In the fall of 1954 the President, who had started his term as an expert on European defense, faced his third Far East crisis since assuming office. This one involved two small island groups off the coast of China: Quemoy and Matsu. When Nationalist forces fled from mainland China to Formosa in late 1949, they left behind substantial garrisons on these two islands. Subsequently, the Nationalists used them as staging areas for harassing the communist mainland and its shipping.

In September the communist (ChiCom) shore batteries shelled Quemoy, and the Nationalists (ChiNats) responded with air raids. Throughout the fall the war of words went on between the opposing Chinese governments. On New Year's Day 1955, Chiang Kai-shek, Nationalist China's president, predicted war at any time. Chou En-lai, Communist Chinese foreign minister, responded that an invasion of Formosa was "imminent." That did not seem likely, given the 150-mile width of the Formosa Strait, the lack of a ChiCom Navy, and the presence of the U.S. Seventh Fleet, which had patrolled the strait since 1950. Still, the war of words accelerated.

On January 28 Congress passed a resolution authorizing the President to react as he saw fit in the defense of Formosa, the nearby Pescadores, and "such other territories as may be determined." Did that include the islands of Quemoy and Matsu? Ike, who had wordsmithed the resolution, wasn't saying. In mid-March Secretary Dulles stated that the United States was prepared to use atomic weapons in the Formosa Strait. This set off an uproar. Since Ike had cleared the statement, he was obligated to defend it—at least initially. A few days later on the way to a press conference he was cautioned by Jim Hagerty, his press secretary, about possible questions on the use of atomics. Ike answered, "Don't worry, Jim . . . I'll just confuse them."[4] He did, too.

By April the crisis was ebbing. Speaking at an Asian-African conference in Indonesia, Chou stressed Chinese friendship for the American people and offered to negotiate disputed matters. Ike responded positively. By the following month the ChiCom shelling of Quemoy and Matsu had eased, and arrangements were made for talks between American and ChiCom officials. Throughout this tense period Eisenhower had listened to conflicting advice: some leaders, such as Chiang Kai-shek and Syngman Rhee, were ready to go to war; others, including the British, thought the two islands should be returned to the People's Republic. Ike had kept his options open and made his own decisions. Would he have used nuclear weapons as advised by Dulles and others? Probably not. Fortunately, Eisenhower handled the crisis so effectively that he was never forced to make that decision.

In early 1955 the Soviets experienced their second change in leadership since Stalin's death: Georgi Malenkov was replaced by Nikolai Bulganin and Nikita Khrushchev — but as First Secretary of the Communist Party, Khrushchev wielded the real power. Soon the new Soviet leadership proposed neutralizing Austria and withdrawing all occupation troops there. There was no disagreement on that from the Western powers, and before long the occupation of Austria ended.

In the meantime Anthony Eden, who had replaced Churchill as British prime minister, and Edgar Fauré, the French prime minister, proposed a summit of the big four, the first since Potsdam in 1945. Dulles had misgivings, and to a lesser degree so did Ike; however, knowing that the public was anxious to reduce Cold War tensions, the United States went along with the proposal. By mid-May the Soviets had accepted the Western invitation, and the summit was scheduled for July at Geneva.

Ike headed for the meeting accompanied by Mamie and John, now an Army major, and a large entourage headed by Dulles. Each side had its objectives: the United States wanted to admit a unified Germany to NATO and the USSR sought recognition of Soviet control of its satellite countries. Not surprisingly, the discussions were not substantively profitable and were often acrimonious. Still, as Samuel Johnson said about a dog's walking on his hind legs: it is not done well, but you are surprised to find it is done at all.

The high point of the summit from the American point of view came on July 21. Looking directly at Bulganin and Khrushchev, Ike spoke sincerely and without notes as he set forth his "Open Skies" proposal. He was suggesting that each side allow the other to employ aerial photography of the other's military facilities. The French and British were enthusiastic. Khrushchev, however, felt otherwise. It would be, he said, nothing more than giving the United States an opportunity to gather target information for a possible attack by American strategic forces.[5] All the Soviets would get in exchange was to confirm something they already knew: the United States had overwhelming strength in nuclear weapons.

The summit ended without either side agreeing to the other's specific objectives. All the same, the frank discussions of Cold War problems, along with the close association of the Big Four leadership over several days, helped create what was later called the spirit of Geneva—an easing of Cold War tensions—felt well beyond the borders of the four countries represented at the summit.

Returning from Geneva with a public approval rating of 79 percent, Ike spent the next several weeks on work connected with the closing days of the 1955 congressional session. Afterward, it was time for a vacation. He and Mamie boarded the presidential plane for Denver, where Ike hoped there would be plenty of fishing and golf. September 23 began as a typical vacation day: morning work on papers from Washington to be followed by an afternoon of golf. That night, though, Ike awoke with what was first thought to be indigestion but by the following day was diagnosed as a heart attack. By that afternoon the President was in an oxygen tent at Fitzsimmons Army Hospital.

Within a couple of days he was resting comfortably while Mamie, installed in an adjoining suite, answered by hand the thousands of get-well wishes sent from all over the country. Vice President Richard Nixon took over the Cabinet and National Security Council meetings in a discreet way, but he faced an informal cabal of "Eisenhower Republicans" who were apprehensive that the vice president might try to gain control of the party apparatus. In a tough position, Nixon had to tread a fine line between seeming uncertain and appearing ruthless.

Ike had a smooth, gradual, recovery, and before long, he was seeing government officials and reading state papers. His Chief of Staff, the laconic Sherman Adams, functioned as Ike's liaison on government matters, while Jim Hagerty, Ike's tough and skilled public relations man, took care of matters in that area. On Veterans Day, November 11, seven weeks after his hospitalization, the President headed for Washington, where he told a cheering crowd at National Airport: "The doctors have given me at least a parole, if not a pardon."[6]

January 1956 saw the new Congress, controlled by Democrats, start the quadrennial partisan debating period preliminary to a presidential election. Complicating matters was the fact that a very popular Republican president had not stated whether he would run again. Although Ike's main concerns were normally foreign and military policy, his State of the Union address that year challenged Congress with many important domestic proposals. These included support for school construction, assistance to depressed industrial areas, improvement of national parks, and "a grand plan" for a speedy, safe, transcontinental highway system.

Ike had been interested in American highways since he participated in the 1919 Army cross-country convoy and had seen for himself the inadequacy of the national highway system. Later, like most other Americans who had fought in Europe, he had been impressed by the German Autobahnen, a superb national highway system permitting high-speed travel. In the summer of 1955 his administration had sponsored a Federal Highway Act that was slowly working its way through Congress. In his 1956 State of the Union address Eisenhower stressed the urgent need for an integrated highway system: by 1970 the number of cars being driven in America would double to 118 million. Ike and Congress differed on how to finance the project, but in the end he gave in to get the bill passed. The interstate highway system resulting from this law became one of Eisenhower's "proudest achievements."

By early 1956 a fully recovered Ike could carry out his presidential duties without any difficulty, and it was now time to decide about running for a second term. Most of his close associates thought that he should, and apparently they helped convince him that he was indispensable. Mamie, who had discussed the matter with Ike's doctor, also supported his running, feeling that he would be better off physically than if he retired to a life of inactivity.

Ike had to try clearing up one other matter before announcing his decision. Some of his associates, in particular Sherman Adams, were urging him to drop Richard Nixon from the 1956 ticket. Ostensibly, this was based on poll results indicating that Nixon would weaken the ticket. Though ambivalent about the vice president, Eisenhower, like most observers, agreed that Nixon was competent and hard working. On the day after Christmas he asked the vice president to drop by for a chat. After citing the poll figures, he opined that perhaps Nixon could strengthen his presidential chances for 1960 by serving in a cabinet post for the next four years. No chance a politician from California would fall for that one. Did Ike believe that the Republicans would be better off with someone else as vice presidential candidate, Nixon asked?[7] Ike did not answer, and there the matter rested for the moment.

In February Eisenhower passed a thorough physical, with the doctors declaring that he should be able to carry on an active life for another five to ten years. At a February 29 press conference he announced his decision: he would run for a second term. As Sherlock Holmes said to Dr. Watson: "The game's afoot."

Chapter 7

Waging Peace

T HE SPRING of 1956 was in many ways the high point of what was later called the Eisenhower equilibrium. Ike had recovered from his heart attack, and there seemed to be little doubt that he would be reelected in November. The country was at peace, Soviet-American relations appeared to be on the up- swing, and most people were better off financially than they had been four years before. After what the country had been through the past quarter-century — the Depression and two wars — the mid-fifties seemed to many to be the Good Years, exuding a sense of well-being and permanence. That was, of course, an illusion.

On June 6, the twelfth anniversary of D-Day, Ike suffered another physical setback. A severe attack of ileitis, an inflamma- tion of the lower intestine, required immediate surgery. After a few weeks in the hospital he emerged looking gaunt, but before the Republican convention in August he was his old vigorous self again. The convention turned out to be a set piece with Ike in un- disputed control. There was still a last-minute flurry concerning the vice presidential choice, drummed up by that perennial can- didate and former boy wonder, Harold Stassen. Shortly before his own nomination on August 22, Ike abandoned equivocating about Nixon and confirmed that the Vice President was again his running mate. The Democrats, meanwhile, had nominated what Eisenhower considered a weak ticket: Adlai Stevenson making a second try, and Sen. Estes Kefauver of Tennessee as vice presidential candidate.

As the 1956 election campaign moved from summer to fall, the public's attention shifted focus from domestic issues to two international crises. The first came in Egypt, at that time ruled by Gen. Gamal Abdel Nasser, a Third World autocrat fairly skilled in playing both sides of the Cold War. Nasser had been negotiating with Dulles for financial assistance to support construction of a high dam at Aswan on the Nile, part of a plan to improve Egypt's industry and agriculture. Favorably inclined toward providing a loan to Egypt for the project, the Eisenhower administration ran into some difficulty with special interests on Capitol Hill. This, combined with some of Nasser's initiatives with the communist bloc, gave Ike second thoughts, and in mid-July he canceled U.S. support for the Aswan project.

As it turned out, Nasser had an alternative plan in mind. About ten days after the withdrawal of American support, he ordered seizure of the Suez Canal, whose annual revenue from tolls, about $25 million, would help on the Aswan project. The reaction in Britain — which operated but no longer garrisoned the canal — was traumatic. British Prime Minister Anthony Eden was prepared to take military action and proposed this to Eisenhower. Ike thought the idea "ridiculous" and said no. At that point Eden, working secretly with France and Israel, designed his own war plan and on October 28 put it into effect. Israel attacked first, driving across the Sinai Desert toward the canal. Within a couple of days British and French bombers went to work on Egyptian air bases, and soon after came a landing of Anglo-French troops at Port Said. Nasser's retaliation came with perhaps the only capability at his disposal, sinking ships in the Suez Canal, thus effectively blocking this shipping route vital to Britain and France.

An outraged Eisenhower was taken completely by surprise at

Eden's war. Interrupting a final election swing through the South, he hurried back to Washington. Then came a new twist: the United States and the USSR, acting jointly, pushed through a U.N. resolution condemning the invasion of Egypt. Eisenhower also ordered an embargo of vital oil shipments to Britain and France. Khrushchev piled on with a threat to destroy the two aggressors with missiles, which no one knew whether real or imaginary. The combination of all this was persuasive enough so that on November 6 (election day in the United States) the British and French and, reluctantly, the Israelis agreed to a cease-fire.

Peaking at the same time as Suez was the crisis in Hungary, probably a consequence of the general loosening of Soviet controls on the satellites after Stalin's death in 1953. In June the anti-Russian riots in Poland had been settled when the Soviets gave the Poles more control over their own affairs. The situation in Hungary was more dramatic: fighting in the streets of Budapest began on October 23 and soon spread throughout the entire country. The American response was vague.

Khrushchev tried some compromises with the revolutionaries, but when Hungary announced that it intended to withdraw from the Warsaw Pact—a defense alliance established by the Soviets with the satellites in 1955—that was too much. In went the Soviet tanks, resulting in 30,000 dead Hungarians and the securing of Soviet rule. Ike handled both crises effectively. In Suez he saved America's allies from further disaster, regardless of how they felt about it at the time. And though in the 1952 campaign he had preached liberating captive peoples, he knew that, short of starting World War III, the United States had no way of intervening in Hungary.

The November 6 election was an overwhelming personal victory for Dwight Eisenhower: 457 electoral votes to Stevenson's 73. Despite Ike's victory, the Republicans were unable to carry either house of Congress, but by then he had become accustomed to working with a Democratic Congress; his administration and the Eighty-fourth Congress had worked together quite harmoniously. After the 1956 elections, the good working relationship between the conservative President and the liberal congressional leaders—Lyndon Johnson in the Senate and Sam Rayburn in the House—continued, at least for the next couple of years.

Eisenhower's second presidential term and final public service offered extraordinary challenges and opportunities. He needed to bring to bear all the talents—poise, introspection, balanced judgments, and decisiveness—developed during a lifetime of remarkable experiences.

In September 1957 he faced one of the most difficult domestic issues: desegregation of schools in Little Rock, Arkansas. A confrontation with Arkansas's governor, Orval Faubus, ended with a presidential order sending in federal troops to effect desegregation. Ike thought that he had handled the matter decisively, but inevitably on this and other civil-rights issues he was criticized for lack of presidential leadership. This criticism was especially directed toward his failure to show personal approval of the Supreme Court's 1954 *Brown v. Topeka* ruling that "separate educational facilities are inherently unequal." Ike felt that a president should never address Supreme Court decisions, but his action at Little Rock turned out to be crucial in the history of civil rights in America, establishing as it did the limits of federal patience on such matters. It was also the first major event in the civil-rights struggle to be aired nightly on television. American whites outside the South gave Ike overwhelming support for his decision to send troops to Little Rock.

The state of the American economy was another domestic problem that Ike, like most of his presidential predecessors, had to face from time to time. A rather sharp recession in 1953 followed the drop in Korean War expenditures, but by 1954 the administration had been able to weather that fairly well. A more severe recession in October 1957 proved to be a sterner test. Unemployment, which had been about 4 percent since 1954, climbed to 7.7 percent by 1958.[1]

Meeting with his economic advisers, including Robert Anderson, who had succeeded George Humphrey as secretary of the treasury, Ike concluded that the chief threat was inflation. This meant bypassing any fiscal remedies that might feed inflationary forces; specifically, Ike accepted his advisers' views to avoid any massive public works program or a tax cut. By the end of 1958 recovery was well under way, but with unemployment remaining high, the Republican Party would pay the price in the 1958 congressional elections. In the end, though, Ike received good marks for the general prosperity during his presidencies, marred only by the two recessions.

Eisenhower's greatest tests and successes in his second term came on the international scene. The most dramatic of these began on the night of October 3, 1957, when the Soviets, using one of their partly developed ICBMs, put into orbit a satellite named Sputnik (fellow traveler). When Americans woke up the next morning to hear a beep . . . beep . . . beep on their radios, many began to be concerned about the country's security. At first, however, Ike paid little attention to Sputnik, calling it a publicity stunt.

It turned out to be more than that, though, with the media and the public. With Sputnik knocking over the image of American technological superiority, U.S. citizens feared for the first time that their homeland was vulnerable to Soviet intercontinental missiles. The public and Congress clamored for committing national resources to regain superiority. From Ike's point of view the United States had never lost superiority, and, as future events showed, he was right.

While some changes in the defense budget were inevitable, the President tried to keep Congress from overreacting. Meeting with Neil McElroy, the new secretary of defense who had replaced Charlie Wilson, he emphasized making budget decisions on real requirements, not public pressure. Preaching to the Defense Department was not enough, though; Eisenhower had to take his prudent approach to the public. Resorting to television, he began a series of "confidence speeches" to help counter public anxiety over the Soviet feat. Two of his talks stressed that the overall strength of the free world was greater than that of the communist countries and that the United States must be selective in expending its resources. Still, the notion of a "missile gap" that Democrats invented during this period survived as an issue throughout his remaining years in the White House.

Ike's planned third speech on the Sputnik controversy was overtaken by another illness. In his office on November 25, 1957, he suddenly felt dizzy and became orally incoherent. He was having a mild stroke. Although his condition soon improved, the symptoms remained for several days. This situation bothered Ike in a way that his previous two presidential illnesses had not. Now sixty-seven years old and worried about presidential disability, he arranged with Richard Nixon just how the vice president would take over if he were incapacitated. No one wanted a repeat of Woodrow Wilson's last year and a half as an invalid president.

In 1958 Eisenhower became involved in a second Nasser-provoked Middle East crisis. For some time the area had been the focus of an arms race, with the United States supplying arms to Saudi Arabia, Iraq, and Jordan, while the Russians were doing the same for Syria and Egypt. In early 1958 Nasser announced that Egypt and Syria were uniting into a new nation, the United Arab Republic, and he then proceeded to orchestrate a media campaign against those Middle East regimes supplied by the United States. Considering the importance of the area's oil to the Western world, there was no question in Eisenhower's mind that preventing any further political upheaval in that area was in America's vital interest.

On July 14, 1958, pro-Nasser forces in Iraq pulled off a coup, seizing power and executing the pro-Western ruler. Radio Cairo urged similar action in Saudi Arabia and Jordan. Ike made a quick decision to commit American forces, and on the following day U.S. troops came ashore in Lebanon. The Americans encountered no pillboxes, only bemused bathers and ice cream vendors. Though potentially threatened, Lebanon was actually a stepping stone for the United States from which to project influence, military or otherwise, into the Middle East. Before long the United States had built up a substantial force in Lebanon, including atomic-capable artillery, as well as Marine units afloat in the Persian Gulf, and an air task force based in Turkey. Ike also asked British Prime Minister Harold Macmillan if he would deploy British troops to Jordan. Macmillan, though a bit dismayed, went along and on the 17th the British flew in a parachute brigade. He couldn't, however, resist reminding Ike that "You are doing a Suez on me."[2]

Nasser was unsuccessful in eliciting Russian support and by late October the threat to the Saudi Arabian and Jordanian regimes seemed over and the last American troops were withdrawn. Ike felt he had accomplished his objective of stabilizing the situation, as well as demonstrating the ability of the United States to move swiftly into the Middle East with military forces. Was there perhaps another outcome that Ike had hoped for but that did not happen: that is, a counterrevolution in Iraq returning a pro-Western government, which might have required the presence of U.S. troops to provide stablity?

As the 1958 off-year election approached, the President had to contend with another problem, this time close to home since it involved his trusted deputy, Sherman Adams. Sherm, as he was called, was well liked within the White House, but by the nature of his duties and personality had accumulated plenty of enemies among Democrats as well as some influential Republicans. In the spring of 1958 Bernard Goldfine, a textile manufacturer and a friend of Adams, was being investigated by federal agencies for some of his dubious dealings. During hearings Goldfine kept invoking Adams's name, which eventually resulted in his being called before a congressional committee.

In his testimony Adams admitted accepting some gifts, including a vicuña coat, from Goldfine but denied using any influence to help him in return. Congress soon broke up for the summer and that seemed to end the matter. But not with a number of influential Republicans who convinced Ike that Adams was hurting the party's already shaky chances in the forthcoming election. That did it, and Adams walked the plank, though there was no perceptible gain for the Republicans. The Democrats, looking forward to 1960, put on a vigorous campaign and on election day the Republicans were trounced: in the new Congress the GOP would be outnumbered by nearly two to one. Nixon's private analysis attributed the rout to Sputnik, the recession, and the Adams affair. Though Eisenhower's personal popularity was undiminished with the American public, the fact was that on Capitol Hill he was a lame duck.

In that same month of November Nikita Khrushchev made a major pronouncement on Berlin. It was, he said, time to end the four-power occupation of that city and transfer control to the German Democratic Republic (GDR) — that is, East Germany, a puppet of the Soviet Union. After that, access to the city would have to be negotiated with the GDR. In case that wasn't clear, he followed through with an ultimatum to the Western Allies: the negotiations for transfer had to be completed by May 27, 1959, or access to the city would be blocked.

Obviously the Soviet position was completely unacceptable to Ike as well as to the leadership of Britain and France. The Western Allies did not consider the GDR a sovereign state, let alone a power to be negotiated with. As the situation became increasingly tense Eisenhower had many sessions with Dulles and his military advisers to discuss possible courses of action. The military proposed employing a large ground force across East Germany to Berlin as a test of Soviet resolve. Ike said no, when the time came a token force would do; if it didn't he would issue his own ultimatum. At a press conference about that time a reporter asked whether the President would employ nuclear weapons. Ike was guarded in his reply, but that was enough for Khrushchev to renew his long-standing demands for a summit. Eisenhower still said no, he did not want to be "dragooned into a summit."[3]

On March 19 Harold Macmillan came to Washington with the mission of changing Ike's mind about a summit. Avoiding a confrontation with the Soviets was a matter of urgency for the British — it would after all, he said, take only eight Soviet H-bombs to destroy England. Meeting with Ike and the terminally ill Dulles the prime minister presented his case, but got nowhere with the Secretary of State and at the time Ike seemed to go along with Dulles. However, after a week of reflection the president decided he might agree to a meeting for the sake of NATO unity, and the Soviets were informed that a summit might be possible.

On May 24 Dulles died, and on the day he was buried, May 27, Khrushchev's ultimatum expired but nothing happened. Dulles's death was a great personal loss for the President but it marked Ike's emergence as his own public secretary of state. Actually he had always called the shots though Dulles generally articulated them publicly.

The new secretary of state, Christian Herter, had a suggestion. Recently Khrushchev had indicated to some visiting American governors that he would like to visit the United States — why not invite him? Ike agreed, and within a week Khrushchev accepted and the trip was set for September. At that point Ike assured Macmillan that this would undoubtedly take the edge off the Berlin crisis.

On September 15 the Soviet premier boarded his plane for the United States with a mission — promoting himself. American officials did not realize it at the time, but Khrushchev's personal position in the Soviet Union was weak and he needed to develop his image as a world figure who was well known and liked, even in America.

After two days in Washington Khrushchev was off to New York, Iowa, and California. The Soviet leader proved to be one of a kind, alternately blunt, clever, humorous, and tough. Even Hollywood was no match for him. His U.S. tour ended in private meetings with Ike at Camp David where nothing much was settled, except that Eisenhower agreed to visit the Soviet Union in 1960 after a May summit in Paris between Khrushchev and the allied leaders. As for Khrushchev's personal mission, the enormous hoopla and publicity attending his every appearance was just what he wanted.

By December Eisenhower was ready to take advantage of the newly available presidential jet aircraft for beginning his own campaign of "personal diplomacy." It turned out to be a nineteen-day triumphal tour of eleven countries in Europe, Asia, and

North Africa. People poured out to see him at every stop; each day's newspapers carried photos of Ike with other world leaders: being greeted by Pope John XXIII at the Vatican; arriving at a formal event with President Ayub Khan in Pakistan; standing next to Nehru and addressing a crowd of more than half a million in New Delhi; waving from an open car next to King Mohammed in Casablanca, Morocco; and meeting with Macmillan, de Gaulle, and Adenauer in Paris.

Having discovered the jet's usefulness, Ike was off again in late February for a shorter jaunt to Latin America, including Puerto Rico, Brazil, Uruguay, Argentina, and Chile. Again, there were huge, friendly crowds and meetings with heads of state. As with the earlier trip, the impression left was one of a well-liked president admired by people worldwide.

An exception, though, was one Latin American country — not visited — where political developments indicated major foreign policy problems for the United States. This was Cuba, now ruled by Fidel Castro, who in January 1959 had led the overthrow of the repressive Batista regime. At first, Castro's takeover in Havana received much popular support in the United States, but this changed as Cuba seemed to be moving under communist hegemony. By the end of 1959 Castro had signed a trade agreement with the USSR and was beginning to portray the United States as an enemy of Cuba. Ike finally became fed up with Castro's anti-Americanism and his communist involvement. Soon after his return from Latin America the President approved a CIA plan to create a force of Cuban exiles for possible use in later guerilla operations against the Castro regime.

By late 1959 the climate was right for a try by Congress to intervene more aggressively in defense matters. Technology was in a state of flux, raising many technical and strategic questions, and few people seemed certain of the answers. The goals of the services were sufficiently far apart so that points of conflict between services or between a service and the administration were well known. With a presidential election now on the horizon, the political situation further encouraged Congress to challenge the administration on both policy and budgetary issues.

What Congress provided was more smoke than fire with inflammatory rhetoric and headlines, but the effect on Eisenhower's defense policy and budget turned out to be negligible. Congressional hearings did expose dissension between the services on both strategic and budgetary issues; however, the public trusted Ike's military judgment. That confidence nullified whatever chances his opponents may have had to change the President's defense programs.

A requirement for an effective nuclear deterrent — the cornerstone of Ike's strategic policy — was target information, particularly about enemy nuclear sites. To meet this need, Eisenhower had in 1954 approved a CIA project for a new type of reconnaissance aircraft, the U-2, with a range of more than five thousand miles and the ability to fly at 70,000 feet. In July 1956, when the aircraft began its flights over the Soviet Union, the USSR immediately protested, charging violations of its airspace. Neither the Soviet nor American publics were, however, told of the flights.

In the early morning of May 1, 1960, a U-2 plane piloted by Francis Gary Powers took off from Peshawar, Pakistan, on a photographic espionage mission covering three thousand miles of the Soviet Union. Previously, the Soviets had not been able to destroy a U-2 but had now developed such a capability and this U-2 was shot down. The CIA assumed that the pilot was dead, but he had been captured relatively unhurt. The Soviets, though, did not reveal that information.

The United States immediately issued a cover story that the plane had gone off course and inadvertently strayed over the Soviet Union. Then Khrushchev sprang the trap, producing the pilot, who had told all. The subsequent international embarrassment to the United States was also felt at home by many Americans shocked by the duplicity of the government's announcements. To Ike's credit, he insisted on accepting complete responsibility and pointed out that all nations conduct espionage within their capabilities. As he said later, "The big error we made, of course, was in the issuance of a premature and erroneous cover story. Allowing myself to be persuaded on this score is my principal personal regret."[4]

The real impact of the U-2 incident came about a week later in Paris at the long-awaited summit meeting of Khrushchev, French President Charles de Gaulle, British Prime Minister Harold Macmillan, and Eisenhower. In short order the Soviet leader terminated the meeting with a shouted tirade against the United States, culminating with the withdrawal of his invitation to Ike for the Moscow visit. The Cold War was on again after a brief intermission.

Ike's final six months in the White House were to some extent overshadowed by the 1960 campaign between Richard Nixon and John F. Kennedy. Although the backgrounds, personalities, and political styles of the two candidates were quite different, they were not far apart on overall goals, hence the campaign tended to focus on means rather than ends.

A good example is in the defense area. Both candidates agreed that the United States must provide whatever resources were necessary for its own defense and adjust spending levels to meet new situations. Kennedy, however, saw a "missile gap" and a decline in power relative to the Soviets, and urged an immediate increase in the defense budget. Nixon's response, strongly backed by Ike—who was understandably sensitive on this issue—was that our military was strong enough to cope with any potential enemy.

The high point of the campaign turned out to be four nationally televised debates between the candidates during October and November. Image was all important, and Kennedy came out best. The election itself was unusually close, with JFK winning the popular vote by just one-quarter of 1 percent. The congressional election was also close, but the Democrats retained both houses by narrow margins.

Assuming the post-election role of caretaker, Ike nevertheless remained deeply involved in certain matters. One such was the 1962 budget. No matter what Kennedy's intentions, Ike intended to leave a balanced budget proposal. He was convinced that his persistence in trying to achieve balanced budgets had played a significant part in the general prosperity of the 1950s.

Another issue about which the outgoing President felt strongly was Cuba. By this time the concept of developing a guerilla force for operations against Castro had evolved into a plan for invading Cuba employing a brigade-sized force of exiles being trained in Guatemala. In early 1961, as one of his last diplomatic initiatives, Ike severed relations with the Castro government. His Cuban legacy to the new administration was thus a CIA plan to use a force of Cuban exiles to invade Cuba and install a provisional government. Whether Ike would have employed the force in the ineffective manner that his successor did is doubtful. Whether he would have employed them at all is unknowable, but questionable.

Nearing the end of his presidency, Eisenhower had good reason to feel that the country was better off than it had been when he took the oath of office in 1953. Certainly that was true in terms of Americans' personal income and living standards. He had also improved the general tranquillity of the country by helping to calm the partisan wrangling of the late 1940s and early 1950s. In the field of civil rights Eisenhower did take some positive steps such as desegregating the District of Columbia and intervening in Little Rock. But in evaluating his contributions to civil rights one is struck not so much by what he did but by what he failed to do: provide strong presidential leadership in furthering racial equality and justice.

Eisenhower's greatest achievements as president came in the area of foreign policy and related defense matters. He ended the Korean War, avoided a confrontation with China over the offshore islands, defused the Suez crisis, and mollified public and congressional overreaction to Sputnik. In other areas, most notably Cuba and Vietnam, he was not as successful, leaving to his less-experienced successor problems that became dangerous in Cuba by 1962 and, later in the decade, tragic in Vietnam.

Despite all his efforts Eisenhower was unable to achieve peace with the Soviet Union. Reflect for a moment, though, on what he did do. The 1950s was a dangerous decade in the Cold War with proliferating weapons increasing the potential for a nuclear exchange between the two powers. Ike handled that challenge superbly, ignoring occasional advice to use or threaten to use nuclear weapons. Knowing better, he had the strength to prevail and still achieve his goals. In the making and managing of strategic policy Eisenhower was a strong, active, and effective president. Equally important was his strong and enduring commitment to principle, to moral purposes, and to abiding human values.

On the evening of January 17, 1961, Eisenhower addressed the nation for the last time as president. His farewell speech was one of the most prophetic statements ever made by an American president. It contained a warning that was to be remembered and restated — though rarely heeded — from then on, giving the language a new and indelible phrase, "the military-industrial complex." This heartfelt admonition was especially surprising coming from an old soldier.

> The conjunction of an immense military establishment and a large arms industry is new in the American experience. The total influence — economic, political, even spiritual — is felt in every city, every statehouse, every office of the federal government.
>
> In the councils of government, we must guard against acquisition of unwarranted influence, whether sought or unsought, by the military-industrial complex. The potential for the disastrous rise of misplaced power exists and will persist.
>
> We must never let the weight of this combination endanger our liberties or democratic processes.[5]

Chapter 8

Afterward and Legacies

AT NOON ON January 20, 1961, John F. Kennedy, the youngest person elected to the presidency, replaced Dwight D. Eisenhower, the oldest to have served in that office. That afternoon Ike and Mamie headed to Gettysburg, Pennsylvania, to begin a new life on the farm they had purchased in 1960. Under Mamie's direction the farmhouse had been extensively remodeled into a large, comfortable home, which was to become the focus of Ike's later years.

Before long, friends and all kinds of visitors began streaming to the farm. While he had hoped for time to play bridge and to catch up on reading, as well as to work on his paintings, he soon found himself busier than ever. As he said a year after he left the White House: "I think I've had more demands made upon me than I've ever had in my life."[1]

Business had to be done, too, including books to be written. He needed as well some systematic way of handling visitors and the pile of correspondence pouring in from all over the world. To facilitate this, he leased a two-story brick building from Gettysburg College as an office. In his status as a former president and as a general of the Army (a rank that technically did not retire), he also had a staff: Robert Schultz, his long-time aide and now a brigadier general; a personal secretary; and, to help in researching and writing his memoirs, his son John, Kevin McCann, and Bill Ewald. Above all, Ike enjoyed having his family near at hand. John and Barbara had purchased an adjacent small home of their own, and to have them and his four grandchildren living nearby was a great satisfaction to Ike.

In the first four years of retirement Ike primarily worked on the two books about his administrations: *Mandate for Change* and *Waging Peace*. While his helpers sorted through a mountain of research documents, Ike would dictate his thoughts on the various topics. Working on a rough draft he would then revise it into final form.

Though thorough and detailed, the books were not particularly exciting. The second volume did, however, receive better reviews than the first. They were a major contribution to history, but little emerged about the central figure himself. That was reserved for a later book, *At Ease: Stories I Tell to Friends.* This informal autobiography contains material not covered in Ike's memoirs or in the earlier *Crusade in Europe.* An excellent book, it gives insights into the man himself, revealing Ike's intellect, character, and ability, as well as his considerable charm.

For years Ike had looked forward to settling down in one place, but, after all those years of moving and action, he found it hard to remain full time in Gettysburg. Golf was still a favorite pastime, so each winter he took a train to Palm Desert, California, where friends provided a home and office. The Eisenhowers also took frequent trips to Georgia, staying in "Mamie's Cottage" on the grounds of the Augusta National Golf Club. In addition, he made various types of business trips. One of the most interesting was in August 1963, when he and Mamie went to Europe with Walter Cronkite to film "D-Day Plus 20." The film shows Ike driving across the Normandy beaches discussing the dramatic days of the assault landing in 1944.

Occasionally the new President requested Ike's advice, beginning with the Cuban problem. Kennedy had first learned of Eisenhower's Cuban invasion plan shortly after the November 1960 election. Throughout the early days of his administration, JFK considered various options, including whether the force should be landed at all. In a decision that he later called "stupid," the new President finally gave the go-ahead to Operation Zapata, an invasion of Cuba by exiles. Starting on Monday, April 17, 1961, it lasted only two days, ending as a complete disaster. All the invaders were either killed or captured.

On April 22 Eisenhower was back at Camp David, at Kennedy's request, to discuss the failed invasion. Ike was particularly amazed that Kennedy had not provided air cover for the operation. JFK responded that he was trying to avoid giving away direct U.S. involvement. Eisenhower was confounded; it was clear that he would never have authorized an unsupported operation despite his earlier approval of the preliminary planning and training.[2]

When the missile crisis came up the following October, Kennedy again consulted Eisenhower, this time during the crisis. Although Ike played no direct part in the decision-making process, he approved of the way that Kennedy, now a more mature president, handled this dramatic confrontation with Khrushchev and the Soviet Union.

On the afternoon of November 22, 1963, Ike was attending a U.N. luncheon when word came of JFK's assassination. He flew immediately to Washington to join Kennedy's family in the East Room as they stood beside the coffin. Soon after, Kennedy's vice president and successor, Lyndon Johnson, called Ike for what was to be the first of many meetings and contacts.

Nixon's defeat in the 1960 election meant that Eisenhower was still the most prominent member of the Republican Party. As a result, he was greatly sought after by some Republicans, especially as the 1964 presidential nominations and election came along. But Ike was never comfortable with the Republican Party after leaving the White House. In 1962 he had tried unsuccessfully to take the party leadership away from the old guard and the

Republican National Committee. Indeed, both during and after his White House years, he had toyed with the idea of forming a third party of moderate Republicans, but nothing resulted from the idea.

The question facing him and other Republicans in 1964 was whom to put up against Lyndon Baines Johnson. Having failed on a bid for the California governorship, Nixon was out. The front-runners then were Sen. Barry Goldwater and New York Gov. Nelson Rockefeller. Not enthusiastic about either, Ike at times tried, though never forcefully, to push some candidates of his own, such as Gov. William Scranton of Pennsylvania. By the time of the convention, however, he conceded that Goldwater would be the candidate. The election results—a landslide for LBJ—were no surprise to Ike.

From the 1964 election until the spring of 1968, Lyndon Johnson dominated public life in an America that was preoccupied with the war in Vietnam and how to deal with it. In early 1965 many options had been open for LBJ, but by that summer he had eliminated all but one—using American troops.

At each of the war's benchmarks—the Rolling Thunder bombing campaign in the north, the troop commitments following, and the conduct of the war itself—Johnson consulted Eisenhower. The President kept Ike informed, sometimes by telephone, sometimes by letter, and sometimes by liaison officials. Ike was supportive of LBJ's decisions, but whether he would have taken the same route as president is another matter.

In November 1965, ten years and two months after his heart attack in Denver, Eisenhower suffered another one. After a hospital stay he was back to some degree of action; still Ike knew what was ahead. A chapel on the grounds of the Eisenhower Library and Museum in Abilene was the place where he and Mamie wanted, when the time came, to be buried alongside their baby Icky. From 1965 on, Ike suffered a series of heart attacks. During the last year of his life he was a patient at Walter Reed Army Hospital in Washington.

In the summer of 1968 Eisenhower dropped any pretense of

Republican political neutrality. At a small news conference in the hospital, the thirty-fourth President strongly endorsed Richard Nixon for the presidential nomination. The next day he had another heart attack, and his health steadily declined.

On Friday morning March 28, 1969, Mamie, John, and David were with Ike in his hospital room. Looking at John, he said, "I want to go; God, take me." In a few hours he was dead. Ike had returned to the heart of America.

FOR TWO decades in the middle of the twentieth century Dwight Eisenhower had found himself in the center of major world events. As a soldier he commanded the Allied Armies that vanquished the Axis forces in the Mediterranean and in Europe. Soon thereafter, he would for eight years lead his country through a perilous period — the Cold War — and keep the peace.

Of the two extraordinary achievements, his leadership in defeating Nazi Germany was the greater. He was able to weld together the armies of different nations into a single coherent fighting force that, along with the Soviet forces, put an end to the Nazi terror. This accomplishment of historic proportions made Ike a world figure, the symbol of that glorious victory. George Marshall put it well in a message to Eisenhower the day after V-E Day.

> This is the greatest victory in the history of warfare. . . . You have been selfless in your actions, always sound and tolerant in your judgments and altogether admirable in the courage and wisdom of your military decisions. You have made history, great history for the good of mankind.[3]

The closing paragraphs of chapter 7 give a brief assessment of Eisenhower's White House years. Overall, he had good reason to feel that the country was better off than when he took office — certainly better than in the decade that followed. He had ended the Korean War and kept the peace in a dangerous time. At home Americans experienced a time of prosperity and contentment, although some might say complacency.

Dwight Eisenhower's legacy is more, though, than the years of peace and prosperity; it is the man himself—that there was such a person of great worth who believed in an essentially good and decent world and who lived a life befitting it. Long after his death and shortly before her own, Mamie was asked what she would like people to remember of Ike. She answered, "His honesty . . . integrity, and admiration for mankind." Perhaps we should leave it at that.

Appendix

Ike's Proudest Achievements as President

On October 18, 1966, Dwight D. Eisenhower wrote a letter to his former press secretary, James C. Hagerty, listing twenty-three of the proudest achievements of his eight-year presidency. The achievements were not in order of importance and were accompanied by Eisenhower's admission that "I had dashed these off the top of my head."

- Statehood for Alaska and Hawaii
- Building of St. Lawrence Seaway
- End of Korean War; thereafter no American killed in combat
- Largest reduction in taxes to that time
- First civil rights law in eighty years
- Prevention of communist efforts to dominate Iran, Guatemala, Lebanon, Formosa, South Vietnam
- Reorganization of the Defense Department
- Initiation, and the great progress in, most ambitious road program by any nation in history
- Slowing up and practical elimination of inflation
- Initiation of space program with successful orbits in less than three years, starting from scratch
- Initiating a strong ballistic missile program
- Conceiving and building the Polaris program, with ships operating at sea within a single administration
- Starting federal medical care for the aged (Kerr-Mills)
- Desegregation in Washington, D.C., and armed forces even without laws

- Fighting for responsible fiscal and financial policies throughout eight years
- Extension of OASI (Old Age Survivors Insurance) to more than 10 million persons
- Intelligent application of federal aid to education (Defense Education Bill)
- Preservation, for first time in American history, of adequate military establishment after cessation of war
- Using federal power to enforce orders of a federal court in Arkansas, with no loss of life
- Goodwill journeys to more than a score of nations in Europe, Asia, Africa, South America, and in the Pacific
- Establishment of the Department of Health, Education and Welfare
- Initiation of plan for social progress in Latin America after obtaining necessary authorization from Congress for $500 million (later called Alliance for Progress)
- Atoms for Peace proposal

Notes

Chapter 1

1. Kenneth S. Davis, *Dwight D. Eisenhower: Soldier of Democracy* (New York: Doubleday, Doran, 1945), 10–11.
2. Davis, *Eisenhower*, 36–37.
3. Dwight D. Eisenhower, *At Ease: Stories I Tell to Friends* (New York: Doubleday, 1967), 4.
4. Eisenhower, *At Ease*, 18.
5. Eisenhower, *At Ease*, 19–20.
6. A good example of this quality is his role as assistant coach of junior varsity football during his senior year at West Point as described by Davis, *Eisenhower*, 145: "The plebes looked up to him, worked hard for him. He had, he discovered, a happy facility for getting men to work for him."

Chapter 2

1. Eisenhower, *At Ease*, 157.
2. Eisenhower, *At Ease*, 166–167.
3. Eisenhower, *At Ease*, 173.
4. Eisenhower, *At Ease*, 181.
5. Eisenhower, *At Ease*, 187.

Chapter 3

1. Davis, *Eisenhower*, 272.
2. Peter Lyon, *Eisenhower: Portrait of the Hero* (Boston: Little, Brown, 1974), 119; Merle Miller, *Ike the Soldier* (New York: Putnam, 1987), 388.
3. Davis, *Eisenhower*, 305. Ike had suggested to Marshall that Gen. Joseph T. McNarney be named as European commander, but McNarney had only recently been named Marshall's Deputy

Chief of Staff. Stephen E. Ambrose in *Eisenhower: Soldier and President* (New York: Simon & Schuster, 1990), 70, makes a logical case for the belief that Marshall had Eisenhower in mind for the job for some time.

4. James L. Stokesbury, *A Short History of World War II* (New York: William Morrow, 1980), 231.

Chapter 4

1. Geoffrey Perret, *Eisenhower* (New York: Random House, 1999), 219.
2. Perret, *Eisenhower*, 237.
3. Ambrose, *Eisenhower*, 118.
4. Roosevelt's dislike of de Gaulle stemmed in part from the general's imperious attitude. While Churchill's backing of de Gaulle kept the French leader's position within the Allied councils shored up, even the Prime Minister complained that the hardest cross he had to bear was the Cross of Lorraine. But there were more important aspects of both leaders' views of de Gaulle that reflected policy differences. In short, they had to do with markets, commerce, and economic power in the postwar world. De Gaulle gave every indication of being a potentially strong French leader when that nation was reconstructed. An important U.S. policy goal for Roosevelt was a France that would not inhibit American penetration of new areas for both resources and markets. The British, on the other hand, wanted a strong postwar France that would help Europe compete economically with the United States. Many books on World War II cover France's relationships with its principal allies on both military and policy matters. For a more extensive development of the thesis set forth above, see for example, Lyon, *Eisenhower*, 152–153 and passim.
5. Perret, *Eisenhower*, 255.
6. John Man, *D-Day Atlas* (New York: Facts on File, 1984), 36.
7. Adam Ulam, *The Rivals* (New York: Penguin, 1971), 4.
8. Dwight D. Eisenhower, *Crusade in Europe* (New York: Doubleday, 1948), 270; Forrest Pogue, *The Supreme Command* (Washington, D.C.: U.S. Government Printing Office, 1954), 192–193.
9. Perret, *Eisenhower*, 319–320.
10. Eisenhower, *Crusade in Europe*, 354–355.
11. Perret, *Eisenhower*, 331.

Chapter 5

1. Joseph E. Persico, *Nuremberg: Infamy on Trial* (New York: Penguin, 1994), 406.
2. Dwight D. Eisenhower, *Mandate for Change: 1953–1956* (New York: Doubleday, 1963), 181.

Chapter 6

1. Douglas Kinnard, *President Eisenhower and Strategy Management* (Lexington: University Press of Kentucky, 1977), 3.
2. Kinnard, *President Eisenhower,* 24.
3. Cited in Eisenhower, *Mandate for Change,* 439.
4. Ambrose, *Eisenhower,* 384.
5. Perret, *Eisenhower,* 527.
6. Perret, *Eisenhower,* 532.
7. Herbert Parmet, *Eisenhower and the American Crusades* (New York: Macmillan, 1972), 424.

Chapter 7

1. Charles Alexander, *Holding the Line: The Eisenhower Era, 1952–1961* (Bloomington: Indiana University Press, 1975), 107.
2. Ambrose, *Eisenhower,* 467.
3. Perret, *Eisenhower,* 575.
4. Dwight D. Eisenhower, *Waging Peace: 1956–1961* (New York: Doubleday, 1965), 558.
5. Eisenhower, *Waging Peace,* 616.

Chapter 8

1. Lyon, *Eisenhower,* 885.
2. Ambrose, *Eisenhower,* 553–554.
3. Ambrose, *Eisenhower,* 201–202.

Select Bibliography

Books on Dwight Eisenhower are innumerable. The following should, I believe, be both interesting and insightful for the general reader who wishes to pursue further the story of Ike and his times.

Alexander, Charles C. *Holding the Line: The Eisenhower Era, 1952–1961*. Bloomington: Indiana University Press, 1975.

Ambrose, Stephen E. *Eisenhower: Soldier and President*. New York: Simon & Schuster, 1990.

Butcher, Harry C. *My Three Years with Eisenhower*. New York: Simon & Schuster, 1946.

Davis, Kenneth S. *Dwight D. Eisenhower: Soldier of Democracy*. New York: Doubleday, Doran, 1945.

Eisenhower, Dwight D. *Crusade in Europe*. New York: Doubleday, 1948.

———. *The White House Years: Mandate for Change, 1953–1956*. New York: Doubleday, 1963.

———. *The White House Years: Waging Peace, 1956–1961*. New York: Doubleday, 1965.

———. *At Ease: Stories I Tell to Friends*. New York: Doubleday, 1967.

Eisenhower, David. *Eisenhower at War 1943–1945*. New York: Random House, 1986.

Eisenhower, John S. D. *Strictly Personal*. New York: Doubleday, 1974.

Ferrell, Robert H., ed. *The Eisenhower Diaries*. New York: Norton, 1981.

Hobbs, Joseph Patrick, ed. *Dear General*. Baltimore: Johns Hopkins Press, 1971.

Lyon, Peter. *Eisenhower: Portrait of the Hero*. Boston: Little, Brown, 1974.

Miller, Merle. *Ike the Soldier*. New York: Putnam, 1987.

Neal, Steve. *Harry and Ike: The Partnership That Remade the Postwar World.* New York: Scribner, 2001.

Parmet, Herbert S. *Eisenhower and the American Crusades.* New York: Macmillan, 1972.

Perret, Geoffrey. *Eisenhower.* New York: Random House, 1999.

Summersby, Kay. *Eisenhower Was My Boss.* New York: Prentice-Hall, 1948.

Index

About the Author

Douglas Kinnard graduated from West Point in the D-Day Class of 1944 and served in combat in World War II, the Korean War, and twice in Vietnam—the latter time as a brigadier general. He retired in 1970 to become a professor-scholar, and after receiving the Ph.D. in politics from Princeton University in 1973 became a member of the political science faculty at the University of Vermont. While there, he took a two-year leave of absence to serve as Chief of Military History, U.S. Army. Since becoming professor emeritus at Vermont he has been a visiting professor at a number of universities. This book is his seventh.